Overcoming the Ordinary Life

Blessings Beyond Barriers

Overcoming The Ordinary Life

Blessings Beyond Barriers

Ann J. Davenport
Carolyn S. Outland

All Scripture references taken from the New American Standard Bible, © 1960, 1962, 1968, 1971, 1972, 1973, 1975, 1977, by THE LOCKMAN FOUNDATION. Used by permission.

Cover picture: Backbone Mountain in East Tennessee.

Overcoming the Ordinary Life
Blessings Beyond Barriers
ISBN 978-1-59872-775-3
Copyright © 2007 Ann J. Davenport and Carolyn S. Outland

Order additional books:
Care Ministries
1518 Kimbro Road
Murfreesboro, TN 37128
615-895-0701
OutlandC@aol.com
www.careministrieschristian.com

All rights reserved. No portion of this book may be used in any form without the written permission of the publisher, except for brief quotations.

Printed in the United States of America.

Contents

Acknowledgements 7

Preface 9

  1. Conformity's Curse 11

  2. Fear Factor 37

  3. Greed's Grasp 63

  4. Religious Retreat 97

  5. Victorious Vessels 135

Conclusion 173

Study Questions. . . . . .Appendix

Note: Each chapter includes two sections. Section One is written by Ann Davenport and Section Two is written by Carolyn Outland.

Acknowledgements

We express deep gratitude to our families for their love and being such a great source of illustrations. Our love for you has taught us, in a small way, the great love God has for all His children.

We want to thank Deborah Pate for editing the manuscript, Lauren Davenport for her help in designing the book cover, and Lu Long for her technical support for the book and in creating our website, www.careministrieschristian.com.

We thank our Sunday school class members and others who have prayerfully and financially supported Care Ministries.

We are filled with gratitude to Jesus Christ who enables us to live an abundant life. To God be the glory!

Preface

It's okay to be ORDINARY, but it's not all right to BE ordinary. Let us explain. God delights in creating and using *ordinary* people, and there are a lot of us! However, He wants to use us in *extraordinary* ways in His kingdom's service to show His presence and power among the nations.

"But we have this treasure in earthen vessels, so that the surpassing greatness of the power will be of God and not from ourselves…" (II Corinthians 4:7)

Unfortunately, many Christians are content to live an ordinary life because of the security and control it seems to bring. This is a deception! God's control does not cease to operate because we refuse to recognize it. God's desire is for us to live an extraordinary life where we acknowledge His control. He then leads us out of our comfort zone and into the unknown, a faith walk of blessings and adventure.

There are many barriers to our faith walk, some self-imposed and some a result of the world system. These barriers are in direct opposition to our spiritual desire to follow God's plan. The key to overcoming the ordinary life and embarking on this walk of faith is total obedience to God, realizing **"in all these things we overwhelmingly conquer through Him who loved us." (Romans 8:37)** The first step in the walk of obedience is to acknowledge God's control over creation and His desire for people to enter a personal relationship with Him through accepting His Son, Jesus Christ.

Life is not always fair, but it can be full. God sent Jesus to be the perfect intermediary between Himself and His people so we might know the Father, understand His plan for us, and live an abundant life of wisdom and peace. Jesus took all our failures and disobedience upon Himself, received our punishment, entered death, and triumphed over it. His resurrection from the grave became the doorway for our entrance into eternity with God in heaven. You stand at a crossroads today. If you have not accepted Jesus as your personal Savior, will you take the first step in overcoming the ordinary life? If Jesus is already your Savior, will you take the first step of radical obedience and make Him your Lord? There are eternal blessings beyond the barriers of ordinary living.

Chapter 1

Conformity's Curse

"And do not be conformed to this world, but be transformed by the renewing of your mind, so that you may prove what the will of God is, that which is good and acceptable and perfect." Romans 12:2

Section 1

Marred in the Potter's Hand

"Arise and go down to the potter's house, and there I will announce My words to you." (Jeremiah 18:2)

One of Carolyn's longtime friends once made the observation, "You and Ann never know where God is going to take you. Your lives are such an adventure!" So it is when we abandon ordinary living and strive to enter God's extraordinary plan for the Christian life. Like an artist, our Creator uses splashes of dark and light to design breath-taking experiences for His children, blessings of worship, service, and pleasure. Of course, what one person might call an adventure of faith, another might describe as a mishap. Carolyn and I have had plenty of those also. When undergoing a mishap or adversity, we should be comforted by the realization our experience is as much a part of God's plan as the events we perceive as pleasant.

As conference leaders, Carolyn and I are frequently called upon to lead weekend retreats. Sometimes these events are held at rustic campgrounds with less than optimal living conditions. While church members may attend only one or two such events a year, we are in retreat settings almost every weekend during the spring and fall, our heavily scheduled time. As leaders, we need to sleep and have pulled-apart time to pray, prepare, and privately evaluate how the event is progressing. After years of sleep deprivation, as retreat attendees partied and enjoyed time away from home and children, we learned to request a separate room at the facility to help us rest and work.

I will never forget a particularly remote campground several years ago. We were the first people to arrive, but a petrified frog in the corner of the meeting room greeted us as we began setting up our media equipment. I am a city girl, born and bred, and any kind of critter pretty much gives me the creeps. This particular frog was especially haunting because he died with his eyes and mouth wide open. In fact, we were not sure he was dead until Carolyn scooped him into a dustpan and discovered he was as hard as a rock! Mr. Frog was the first of several "adventures" we would experience on our weekend retreat.

I noticed there was one private room in the facility adjacent to the meeting room and on the same level as the kitchen. All the other beds were upstairs in a large dormitory. I quickly moved our suitcases into the privacy of the downstairs bedroom before anyone else arrived and attempted to claim it. This tiny room was equipped with a unique bed, double sized on the bottom bunk with a single bunk on top. I did not care about the bed; I was elated we would be downstairs while the all-night party people were upstairs.

The evening meal was delicious, session one went smoothly, and all was well until bedtime. Carolyn and I had our evaluation session and began to prepare for well-deserved rest. I looked at the top bunk and decided I was afraid of the altitude. Carolyn, not wanting to climb up and down either, suggested we sleep together in the bottom bunk since it was a double size. I agreed, and we both climbed into bed. Not wanting to disturb Carolyn, I was trying to make as little noise or movement as possible; but this bed was immensely uncomfortable. In fact, it felt as if my rear end was resting on the floor! Suddenly, there was a horrendous noise; the midsection of the mattress and two wooden slats had collapsed to the floor. Shocked, but unhurt, we managed to climb out of the mattress and examine our situation. There were six slats holding up the bed, and the two middle ones had dropped to the floor.

"We are blessed this happened," explained Carolyn. "That's why our rear ends were sagging to the ground. We can straighten these two slats, and we'll be good to go for the night." I found her explanation to be somewhat reassuring at the moment. We replaced the two slats, moved the mattress into place, and climbed back into bed. Even more apprehensive about moving around, I tried to be still, fearing more consequences. We both drifted off to peaceful sleep.

WHAM! The two sleeping beauties were suddenly folded up in the mattress like a bologna and cheese sandwich. All six slats had collapsed, and we found ourselves with our knees touching our foreheads! Everywhere we turned was mattress. I weakly said, "What do we do now?" Carolyn said, "Let me think. The first step is to get my knees off my forehead so I can think." I was not laughing at her attempted humor.

After laboring for some time, we finally extricated ourselves from the mattress and began to survey our situation. "I AM NOT getting back on those slats," I exclaimed. "Well, the only alternative is to move the mattress to the floor," Carolyn responded. "Okay, anything is better than what we've been through!" We laid the mattress on the floor, but there was one problem. It completely blocked the door, so it was impossible to leave the room. "What if I have to go to the bathroom during the night?" I asked. "You better go try now," Carolyn sternly warned, "Once this mattress is down for the night, we're not getting back up." Like a child, I trudged off to the bathroom; we finally settled down again to sleep.

Suddenly, I remembered Mr. Frog. "Carolyn, what if there are frogs in here? We're on the floor now; they may try to sleep with us." "Just go to sleep. I'm sure that was the only one and besides, they are more afraid of us than we are of them." Somehow I did not believe her, but I was too tired to argue.

We were awakened early the next morning by a shriek. "THERE'S A SNAKE IN THE SINK!" The kitchen crew had arrived downstairs only to discover Mrs. Snake and her baby snakes nestled in the kitchen sink about eight feet from our door. Suddenly, Mr. Frog did not seem so bad!

God takes all the events of our life, the humorous, the sad, the troublesome, and the happy ones and molds them into the artistry of a human being. He is the Master Potter who is in control of the elements and experiences. Unlike people, His hands and His heart can be trusted.

National news recently covered the story of a teenage girl who decided to celebrate her eighteenth birthday with a body piercing. She went to a local shop and had a ring placed in her left breast. Within a few weeks, she was in agony and reported to the local emergency room. After quick examination, the alarmed doctors found she had an acute infection. It was so widespread she had only hours to live. The only choice she had was to lose her left breast or die. Her shocked family demanded a second opinion. They were told there was no time for another opinion, and the young woman was rushed to surgery. She survived the initial infection only to offer this advice, "Be sure you check out someone before you allow them to touch your body." Good advice. We need to check out the hands before they begin changing us!

Body piercing, neon hair and tattoos are just a few of the challenges today's parents encounter with their teens. Parental nagging of all generations has elicited the same response, "I've just got to be me." Sounds good, but place twenty teenage girls in a room, each wanting to be an individual, and notice how much they look alike. We can laugh (or cry) at how teenagers bend to the latest fashions, but adults, even Christians, have succumbed to the "conformity curse." Unfortunately, instead of being a peculiar people, we have adopted the world's standards, lifestyles, politics, and fashions. We pretty much handle our lives on a daily basis like non-Christians around us, paying little attention to the forces molding us.

Have you seen the child's toy, Silly Putty? It is so flexible it can conform to any shape. The texture allows it to pick up newsprint so sentences can be read on the putty if laid on the ink. Like this child's toy, we conform to the ideas we encounter and pick up our impressions from the world system. We are Silly Putty people.

God desires to transform His people into the image of His Son rather than Christians conforming to the world system. He fashions us as vessels of service to contain and carry the message of the Gospel. Perhaps no other illustration in the Bible gives us as clear a picture of the sovereignty of God and His desire to mold us as Jeremiah 18:1-6, the story of Jeremiah's visit to the potter's house.

The Potter's Sovereignty

"Behold, like the clay in the potter's hand, so are you in My hand." (Jeremiah 18:6b)

Creation

Clay is shapeless, ugly and gray, without power to change itself. The clay represents people, frail humanity. Pastor James Merritt explains, "Clay by itself is useless, but it is not worthless. Clay is like gold to a potter." The Potter appears, scoops it up, molds the clay and begins to work it on His wheel. He is patient, molding and remolding the clay until He produces vessels fit for His Kingdom's service. His hands are pure and loving. He does not mar and mangle; He makes and fashions.

God's creative process far exceeds the most gifted sculptor. He creates each person as an individual work of art, beautiful and equipped for unique assignments and relationships. Growing up in Southeast Alabama, I was the second daughter in a family of three children. I have jokingly said my parents would have had eight children if the first seven had been girls; they were intent on having a son. When my brother, James Ed, was born, the family was complete.

We were middle class in our culture and family background, but economically poor. If you are considered poor in Alabama then you are *really* poor. My mother's desire was for all three of her children to take piano lessons, but she and my father could not afford it. Uncle Jim, Mom's brother, was a longtime bachelor, a pharmacist, and still lived with his parents. My mother convinced him to pay for his nieces and nephew to have piano lessons. Miss Hagood, the piano teacher, attended our church, and she taught us how to play using gospel hymns.

My sister, Becky, and I were soon in demand to play for Sunday school classes, civic clubs, and worship services at surrounding churches. However, I was disappointed we became known as the "Johnson girls." People did not bother to learn our first names; if they did, we were constantly being called by the wrong name. It was as if we were interchangeable. If one of us could not play, then the other would do. I enjoyed serving through music, but I soon became irritated when people viewed me as a *pianist*, not a *person*. The divine Potter is different. He knows everything about the individual, calls people by name, and loves with an inexhaustible flow of compassion. To experience the higher calling of the extraordinary life, He asks us to do the same. As we love people, we become creators along with our Lord, creators of Godly relationships, each as unique as the people involved.

Years ago, I took my children to the aquarium in Chattanooga, Tennessee. We strolled from level to level, observing huge tanks of fish and other sea life. My imagination was captured at one tank containing a school of gorgeous, graceful fish, darting rapidly through the water. In the same tank was one plain turtle paddling awkwardly and slowly to the center of the tank. Suddenly, the turtle emerged from the water, climbed up a rock, and began to walk on an island. It dawned on me his unique, and to some eyes, ugly design enabled him not only to swim but walk on land, something the elegant fish could not do.

Our Potter designs Christians, like the turtle, to walk on a higher plane. Yes, we are in the world, as the turtle was in the water, and by the world's standards a spiritual Christian may appear awkward and well…peculiar. However, God has equipped His people to be lifted to a spiritual level and walk with the Lord in an extraordinary adventure of faith. The world can neither perceive nor understand the higher calling of a Christian.

Discipline

In addition to making us, the Potter is continually remaking us as the need arises. This is God's discipline that operates as surely as His creation process. God gives parents the same responsibility of molding their children through discipline. In 1990, our family lived in a two-level house with a steep incline to the backyard. From the top of the roof to the asphalt driveway in the back was at least a 35-foot drop. One Saturday afternoon, I was cleaning house on the living room level when I heard footsteps running across the roof. To my dismay, I realized my twelve-year old daughter and nine-year old son were missing from the house. I ran down the back steps into the driveway and gazed upward to see Michelle and Rad racing as fast they could back and forth across the roof. They had swung out on an old CB radio tower adjacent to the second story deck, climbed onto the roof, and were having the time of their lives!

Knowing one of them would soon encounter death, I began to scream, as any good mother would do, "Come down from there right now. You are going to fall and break your necks!" My more compliant son immediately began to descend the tower, and Michelle reluctantly followed. I raced back inside, met them on the deck, and continued my motherly discipline. "What in heaven's name were you thinking? You could have fallen and killed yourselves. Don't ever let me catch you doing such a thing again!"

Rad hung his head, but Michelle immediately shot back, "And what will you do if we try it again?" I was stunned and dumbfounded that my status as mother was being challenged, especially in light of the danger. All I could blurt out was "It's so bad; you really don't want to know. Just don't make me tell you."

Unlike earthly parents, when it comes to discipline, God is never at a loss for words nor is He short on ideas. He takes the marred vessel, places it back on the Potter's wheel and remolds it to His liking. The knowledge of God's discipline should bring comfort to the Christian. When he makes a wrong decision or willfully sins, the Potter continues to work with him as a loving parent.

"For those whom the Lord loves, He disciplines, and scourges every son whom He receives." (Heb 12:6)

Freedom of Choice

God creates and molds His children, He disciplines and remolds them, but His greatest use of sovereign power is when He gives people the freedom to choose. God makes us, but He does not manipulate us. We are not puppets. God has imparted to people some of His power as they decide whether or not to be His vessels and whether they will choose daily to follow His plans rather than their own. This limit on God's power does not diminish Him. It is His gift to His creation. Non-Christians, as well as Christians, are able to exercise their freedom, and it is a tremendous responsibility. Choices bring consequences, and consequences are our responsibility.

How have Christians handled this shared power over their lives? Sadly, most have responded with dissatisfaction. Unlike the Psalmist in **Psalm 139:14, "I will give thanks to You for I am fearfully and wonderfully made,"** many are unhappy with their condition. There has been an explosion of cosmetic surgery in the United States in the quest for beauty and acceptance. Many desire to remake themselves. We are unhappy with our weight, our intelligence, our positions, and our financial status. People in this country have allowed themselves to be defined by the kind of automobiles they drive, the size houses they inhabit, or the brand of clothes they wear. I heard a statistic recently the average home in the U.S. is now 2,300 square feet compared to 1,300 square feet in 1970. We have twice the living space, but I doubt we are twice as happy. Many of us, especially so-called committed Christians, have squandered our God-given power to choose by making the wrong choices.

If people are honest, most would confess materialism brings more problems and obligations than joy. Carolyn tells a humorous story about her sister-in-law who purchased a new van with all the bells and whistles. She was so proud of her purchase; she wanted to keep it immaculately clean. While driving one day, enjoying the fresh air with her moon roof open, she pulled up to the automatic carwash. After paying for the carwash, she pulled in, forgetting her roof was still open. As the soapy water began to pour onto her head, she reached for the button to automatically close the roof and, instead, hit the button that opens the windows, just as the soap arm went down the side of the van. Thoroughly wet and confused by this time, she kept hitting buttons and managed to open the doors just as the water spray came back down the sides of the van. Embarrassed and soaked at this point, she pulled out, left the carwash, and raced home to vacuum the water out of the van before her husband could see what she had done!

The Potter's Purpose

God has made people for a higher purpose than acquiring and maintaining material possessions, and we can live in the blessings of His purpose. To do so, God must be allowed to govern our choices. People have no control over their race, their family, or their birthplace, but God does; and He uses these factors to His glory. The unique personalities, appearance, and gifts we possess are part of God's design for Kingdom service. Simply put, He wants us to produce spiritual results as we witness to others of His presence and saving power. The living demonstration of His leadership in our lives constitutes the purpose for our being here and explains why He designed us the way He did.

However, like a child chasing an elusive butterfly, many people aimlessly search for fulfillment. A friend of mine from church is a long-time educator and conducts parenting conferences on a regular basis. Nancy begins each conference by asking the parents what they most want for their children. She shared that the overwhelming answer from parents is they want their children to be happy. There is little interest in holiness, service in God's kingdom, or even for the child to seek God's will. She advocates the parents pray for their children to be Godly, and then goodness and joy will naturally follow. Her advice is good for adults, too, because in our activity-filled lives, we often neglect the true purpose for our existence: to be a living demonstration of God in our life and lifestyle.

Recently, Carolyn and I spent several hours shopping at the local mall. We decided to take a break and approached a cookie shop. The store occupied a small square footage, but there were five employees working. One was in the kitchen area baking, one was chatting on the telephone, and three young people were in the display area arranging the warm cookies behind the glass. We walked to the left side of the display area and began talking about our selections. Several minutes went by as the employees continued to arrange cookies, but no one offered to wait on us. Growing a little impatient, I decided we needed to move over to the right side of the store toward the cash register, assuming that was where the orders were taken. We walked to the other side and continued to wait several more minutes. The cookies smelled wonderful and looked even better, but still the employees neglected to sell us one.

Finally, growing a little irritated, I commented, "Those cookies sure do look good." "Yes, they do," replied one of the workers. Amazingly, there was no offer to help. "Do you really sell those cookies?" I asked. With a look of genuine surprise, the employee replied, "Of course, would you like one?" I finally was able to place an order, pay for it, and sit down with Carolyn to eat our cookies.

We immediately began to analyze our experience and realized as Christians and church members, we were much like the cookie store employees. We are engrossed with our church jobs and arranging Christian programs and fail to offer a spiritually hungry world the Bread of Life. Our non-Christian friends are observing our lives and many times desiring the faith we exhibit. We fail to put our activity-driven lives aside long enough to engage them in a dialogue about their feelings and desire for something deeply meaningful. In the failure to share Christ, we miss our God-given purpose for being.

Busyness and neglect are benign explanations for our behavior. It is SIN that mars God's purpose in life. The Potter is not at fault in the way He made us. Our rebellion against His purposes mars us in His hand, but God can take the ruins of our life and remake it into something beautiful. I love **II Corinthians 5:17, "Therefore, if anyone is in Christ, he is a new creature; the old things passed away; behold new things have come."** God is the God of new things and they occur daily.

As we travel leading conferences, people question Carolyn and me about how we met and began our ministry. For me, our ministry began in 1986, with a prayer the Spirit impressed into my heart. I prayed for a friend, one who loved God above all other things. Somehow I sensed if this person loved God above all other things, and if I loved God in the same way, our friendship could survive any circumstance or problem. Little did I know what I would face in a few short years. Carolyn had been praying for a best friend for ten years and was discouraged, questioning if there was such a person for her life.

I was so confident God would answer the prayer He inspired; I began examining every woman who entered my life asking, "Is she the one?" In August of 1986, I sensed I had met my God-given friend. Carolyn and I were serving on the state board of the woman's organization for our denomination. We lived forty-five miles apart but began riding together to the state meetings. There was an immediate spiritual bonding that far exceeded our expectations. We began leading conferences at the same events and then began a joint conference-leading ministry.

In 1990, just as we planned to launch a full promotion of Care Ministries, my marriage of eighteen years came to a tragic end through divorce. Two and a half years of counseling, two children, church membership, many prayers, and twice as many tears, were not enough to save the marriage. My immediate family, other than my two children, resided out of state; my God-given friendship with Carolyn became a lifeline of encouragement and Christian support.

Divorce can be compared to your house burning down with you in it. It carries a pain and stigma unlike other family tragedies because some people want to assign blame and do so without knowing the truth behind the situations judged. Emotional and financial burdens are heavy with single parenting, and strife between partners does not end with a piece of paper saying it is over. My life was marred in the Potter's hand, but He had already set about remaking me.

I immediately went to work full time, teaching business in public school. This placed Care Ministries on hold as I made numerous trips to court. After more than two years, I was still awaiting a property settlement from the Court of Appeals in Nashville. I cannot describe the depths of my weariness and discouragement. Emotional turmoil became a physical sensation similar to having my skin burned constantly with low heat. The children were visiting their father one afternoon in October of 1992. Exhausted from working full time and balancing the responsibilities of single parenting, I fell into bed for a short nap. I awoke a little later, my mind bursting with a word, one word over and over again raced through my thoughts–*pristine*. The thought continued on and on for several minutes. I was not sure what the word meant, so I reluctantly pulled myself out of bed, headed to the office to find Webster's dictionary. Pristine means pure, in a virgin state. I was confused. How could a woman married for eighteen years with two children be considered a virgin? At the same time, God's Spirit continued to reassure me this was His message for me.

Two days later, I understood a little more when the legal papers arrived from the court, all stamped with the date of my "pristine" experience. The legal aspect of the divorce was finished. I was reminded of **II Corinthians 5:17, "old things passed away, new things have come."** Spiritually, I was new, pure, with a God-given purpose. I am pristine; I refuse to be deformed and crippled by the label of "divorce." I am assured of my remolding by the Potter's hands. This is not only my good news; it is the good news of the Gospel. Our future is not defined by our defeats. It is decided by the remolding of the Potter. *We are what He says we are, not what the world labels us to be.*

The Potter's Nature

On that October afternoon in 1992, I learned more about the nature of the Potter. He is a loving Father who sustains us through the emotional upheaval of a family breakup. He is also a God of details. The decision from the court was finalized exactly twenty-one years from the date my husband and I were engaged to marry. I was more confident than ever God was remolding my life to fit His purposes.

I had personally encountered the same wise, patient Father the prodigal son found in Luke chapter 15. *The Prodigal Son* challenges every perception of God as a stern, distant judge, ready to hand out quick punishment for human transgressions. Instead, we find a patient, long-suffering Father who waits for His marred child to come to his senses, exercise his freedom to choose, and return to His hands.

After squandering his resources and suffering deep humiliation, the son returns home, requesting the father make him a hired servant; but the father has a better idea. He remakes him as a leader in the household, a beloved son. Many times we approach the father with prayers of "give me," when he is waiting to hear us say, "Please, Father, make me into your servant." What a wonderful father who says, **"...this son of mine was dead and has come to life again."** The personality of the Potter is one of mercy, forgiveness and love for those who will repent and return to His hands. If we decide to stay in the far country, He allows us to stay. But His love continues to woo us home. He watches, waits, and weeps, just as we do when our children are in the far country, not condoning but loving all the while.

"The Lord's lovingkindnesses indeed never cease, for His compassions never fail, they are new every morning. Great is Your faithfulness." (Lamentations 3:22-23)

The curse of conformity is that it exalts the world system and molds us into something other than what God intends. We miss His spiritual blessings, which are eternal, because we are investing in the temporal. He gives, and the world system encourages us to take and keep. Even as I desire to follow Him closely and reflect His image, God has a way of showing me how selfish I can be.

Carolyn and I led a weekend retreat for a women's ministry group in a large church near Memphis. Carolyn ate at the table with a young woman who shared about being the first member of her family to become a Christian. She had been led to the Lord by an in-law. She had no Bible and no church affiliation, but she suddenly knew the Lord and had a new relationship. The woman had purchased a used car, and the previous owner left an old Bible in the back window. As this lady was cleaning her car, she found the Bible, sun-bleached and water damaged. However, it was the only one she had, so she carried it to church with her the next Sunday.

The young woman wandered into church and sat next to an older lady. The kindly woman helped her find the announced scripture. Sometime during the service, the older woman nudged her and said, "You really need a good Bible. Take mine." The young woman was surprised by the offer but accepted it. She thought she would shop the next week and replace the Bible before Sunday. She found an identical Bible, but to her dismay, she discovered it cost $100. She could not afford to replace it, but that is not the point of the story. Rather, it is the kindly woman who had freely given away her $100 Bible to a young woman she had never seen before that day.

As Carolyn told the story, I reached down and lovingly took my Bible into my arms. I am 54 years old, and I had, for the first time in my life, a $100 Bible. Mine is leather, with a lifetime guarantee, gold edged pages, with cross-references and concordance. "Please, Lord, I prayed silently, don't make me give my Bible away."

I immediately was filled with conviction from the Spirit as He spoke: "I have given you all things, including the life of my Son." I knew at that moment how marred I am in the Potter's hand. The good news is He is constantly remolding me on His wheel.

"But the vessel that He was making of clay was spoiled in the hand of the Potter..." (Jeremiah 18:4)

The good news of the Bible is God does not give up on us because we are imperfect. He does not throw us away when we are marred. He uses all the circumstances of life to draw us to the Potter's wheel, and He continues to work on our hearts. My deepest desire is that I will not be like child's putty but rather like molding clay, allowing God to bend and shape me to His will. I am confident if I allow Him, the Potter will shape me into a spiritual vessel useful for service.

"And do not be conformed to this world, but be transformed by the renewing of your mind, so that you may prove what the will of God is, that which is good and acceptable and perfect." **(Romans 12:2)**

Section 2

He Remade the Vessel as He Saw Fit

As Ann and I began to write this book, a Godly couple in East Tennessee invited us to housesit for them while they were on vacation. Harry and Vickie Ford opened their home to us for a week in October. We readily accepted the offer, especially since God's handiwork is on display in the colorful mountains during this time. Their only request was for us to feed two cats, a big dog and most importantly, a herd of goats. We were confident we could transform ourselves from city women to goat raisers without much difficulty. We arrived at the Ford's house before they left so Harry could train us in tending goats. All went well.

However, our first day of feeding did not go as smoothly. The goats were very hungry and began to push each other and then push us. The horns on the Billy goat began to look larger and larger the closer he came. Actually the goats were quite well behaved, which surprised us completely. They just wanted food and wanted it immediately!

The dog was another story. He was a Giant Pyrenees and he lived up to his name of a GIANT. He was solid white, very playful and took a real liking to me. We determined because I also have white hair, he felt a real connection. In fact, Ann said she thought he had fallen in love. I cannot deny he was attracted to me! He nuzzled up and smeared "nasal fluid" all over my shirt. Ann said she thought she was going to throw up! When it was time to put the big dog back into the fenced area with the goats, he refused to go. After much pushing, pleading and praying, we finally managed to get him pried away from me and into the barnyard. Thank God for answered prayer!

Every day brought a new challenge, including rain. We borrowed Harry's rubber boots, which almost reached our hips. We trudged to the goat pen walking like Frankenstein because our knees would not bend in the boots. The sight scared the goats worse than the goats scared us. Not wanting to get our hair wet, we carried umbrellas, another shock to the goats' mental health. We were probably the only "farmers" who fed a herd of goats under an umbrella.

We attempted to dress the part of goat raisers by wearing boots, denim shirts and carrying big sticks. But our bravado was betrayed by our actions. When the goats or the dog would brush their muddy bodies against us, we would yell, "YUCK." This was not the usual vocabulary for natural born goat raisers! We had to fight the urge to place some tranquilizers in their food. Regardless of how much we may have dressed like goat raisers and performed the duties of goat raisers, we were just pretending to be goat raisers.

In the same way, God's children often dress like committed Christians and may even perform the duties of Christians. However, their hearts and lives betray them. Christians living the ordinary life pretend to be useful vessels God has made. They pretend to love when they are shallow in their concern, pretend to be servants when they often refuse to obey, pretend to be committed when commitment basically means attending church services, and pretend to be burdened for the lost while keeping the Good News to themselves. This pretense may go unnoticed by others but it is seen clearly by the all-knowing eye of God.

As the Holy Spirit works in the Christian's life, this pretense becomes obvious. The marred Christian is like the world in the desire for "things" and conformity to worldly standards. Ask yourself this question, "Is my life <u>radically</u> different from a good, moral non-Christian?" If one is honest, the realization is clear there is a need to be remade.

Are you willing to be remade into a useful vessel as God sees fit? Are you willing to ask God to remake your children or grandchildren into His image? All of us would probably answer, "Yes," to that question. However, we want the process to take place without struggle, heartache and pain. How does this mesh with the storms of life that come our way or into the lives of our children? Little of what Jeremiah said to the people of his day was what they wanted to hear. He warned them of coming days filled with difficulties and trials. This admonition clashed with their wish list of prosperity, peace and security. How much of your prayer life consists of requests for prosperity, peace and security for yourself and your children? God's concerns are much simpler. God wants His people to learn to trust Him, to desire His will more than their own. How do you become a vessel God can use?

Willing to Be Crushed

We do not learn to completely trust God when things are going smoothly. We learn by being stretched beyond our natural abilities and comfort. Have you ever watched a potter as he works the clay? The clay is pounded, pushed and seemingly abused. Being remolded as God's vessel seldom feels pleasant. Facing the storms of life is not an easy experience for any of us. When we are going through a difficult time, we need to realize we are on the Potter's wheel. Often it is our children who are on the Potter's wheel. There is a great temptation, especially for mothers, to reach out and deliver their children from the turmoil and pain of being remade by the Potter. We do not want to see them hurt and motherly protection can hinder the work of the One who loves them most. We must realize God is the designer of our lives and our children's lives. Rest assured, God only does what is best. Don't despair. *His intentions are for the marred vessel to become a better vessel.*

Crushed? None of us like the process of being crushed. Someone has said every adult you meet has experienced a broken heart. God uses our broken hearts to prepare us *for* His heart and then to *be* His heart in a hurting, lost world.

As we are crushed, we lose our pretense of perfection. Have you been around someone whose life seems absolutely perfect? Their children are blameless, their homes are immaculate, their spouse is a servant and all is right with the world. The truth is this: we are far from perfect and we must be willing to admit it. No one is drawn to Jesus Christ by seeing our façade of perfection. Others are drawn to the Lord when they see our faith in a time of tragedy and trouble.

"But we have this treasure in earthen vessels that the surpassing greatness of the power may be of God and not from ourselves. We are afflicted in every way but not crushed; perplexed but not despairing; persecuted but not forsaken; struck down but not destroyed." (II Corinthians 4:7-9)

- Are you being crushed?
- Do not concentrate on the storm in your life.
- Trust the God of the storm to bring good from it.

My daughter, Jenise Castle, was crushed by infertility for years. She had exhibited an overwhelming love for children all her life. She and her husband, Wade, prayed for her to get pregnant, but to no avail. Our church prayed and, of course, I prayed for her every day. I never realized the deep agony infertility brings to a woman until I saw my daughter struggle with this burden. Jenise's doctors tried everything known to modern medicine to enable her to conceive, including invitro fertilization. Following the IVF procedure, the doctor felt sure three embryos would live. I remember clearly when Wade called to report on the test concerning the health of the implanted embryos. All had died. I could hear Jenise whimpering like a little, hurt kitten and it broke my heart. As Jenise's mother, it was impossible to see her hurt so deeply and not feel the same hurt.

After numerous disappointments resulting from the failed infertility treatments, the emotional turmoil was too great. Jenise and Wade decided God did not want them to have a baby. With much anguish, they determined to make the best of their broken dreams. They were crushed, but in the process they were learning to trust the Hand of God.

God gave me several scriptures over the years concerning Jenise. He assured me through His Word she would have a child. One particular scripture spoke to my heart.

"He makes the barren woman abide in the house as a joyful mother of children. Praise the Lord." (Psalm 113:9)

With each failed treatment, the possibility of this promise being true looked bleak. However, I would open my Bible to these scriptures and be strengthened in my faith.

God gave another assurance after the failure of IVF. One morning in my quiet time, I was given a mental picture of an infant boy's outfit and God directed me to go buy it as an act of faith. For months, I searched for it in several cities. Although I found many cute infant clothes, they were not the one God had shown me. Finally, I saw the exact outfit hanging on the wall of a local store. I bought it and kept it in a spare closet. Each day for two years, I would go to the closet, hold the outfit toward heaven and pray God would fulfill His promise. This action was totally irrational from the human point of view. Although my human spirit was crushed by my daughter's hurt, my Spirit was renewed every day by God's promise. In the face of crushing disappointments, I continued to assure Jenise of God's plans for her. Praise God, Jenise kept a strong belief the Potter had a purpose in His crushing disappointments. She had learned to trust what she could not understand and so had I.

Wade and Jenise considered adoption and foster parenting. Yet every time they began the process, it seemed as if God was telling them, "No." However, on March 8, 2004, my son-in-law received a call from Dr. David McKnight, a fellow church member. David was a part of the men's prayer group, along with Wade, and was also an obstetrician. David asked Wade, "Do you and Jenise want a baby?" Taken by surprise, Wade answered, "You know we want a baby." David asked, "Today?" He explained a woman had walked into the local hospital in labor but due to personal problems could not take the baby home. The woman had chosen to give the baby life but needed a good home for him.

Wade called Jenise and explained the situation. They knew nothing about the baby's overall health, sex or race. However, after praying for wisdom and guidance, they knew this was God's plan for their life. The next day, they brought home a beautiful, 4 lb. 10 oz. baby boy. He was a blue-eyed blond, with an amazing resemblance to his adoptive parents. They named him Luke and the little bundle in a blanket was a clear example of God's faithfulness. The years of waiting on God's promise culminated in a wonderful gift straight from His heart. Words cannot express the elation that filled our hearts. In fact, Jenise said the joy of Luke had taken away her deep desire to become pregnant.

Wade and Jenise gave me the information they wanted to include in a birth announcement and asked me to write a poem:

GOD'S DELIVERY

Our lives changed forever on March eight,
It was God's design and not just fate
We were at work and a phone call came,
A baby was born, needing the Castle name.
Our routine shaken, our minds all a flutter,
Could we become a Daddy and Mother?
At first glance, we were filled with love,
He was our son, a gift from above
A true fulfillment of God's perfect plan,
Delivered to us by His loving hand.

Luke has been a tremendous blessing to our family. In addition, he has been a blessing to the members of our church because many people prayed for this child. Those who labored in prayer have a special attachment to Luke because they had a part in giving him life. Our church has a service in which parents and baby are dedicated to the Lord. For his dedication, Luke wore the infant outfit that hung in my closet for two years, awaiting the fulfillment of God's promise. From a crushing experience, God brought a contagious excitement. Members of our church were encouraged in their personal faith as they saw God's faithfulness. God works in mysterious ways, showing His ability to bring His blessings through the most unusual means.

- Have you encountered a crushing disappointment in life?
- Do you question why God has allowed hurt to overwhelm you at times?
- Crushed?
- Trust.

Willing to Be Compliant

If we are going to be made into a vessel God can use, we must be compliant to His purpose. The Master Potter does the molding but our attitude often determines the length of the molding process. Why do we fight against God's purposes in our lives? It would be much better if we were intentionally compliant in the Potter's hands.

Unfortunately, sometimes we comply but it is a forced compliance. I heard an account of an elderly couple celebrating their fiftieth anniversary. A reporter visited them for an interview. It seems this couple's compatibility was well known in the small community. In fact, it was rumored they had never had a disagreement or argument. The reporter asked the husband if the rumor was true. The elderly gentleman confirmed it was indeed true. Upon further examination, the husband began to explain their fifty years of marital harmony.

He related he and his new bride went to the Grand Canyon on their honeymoon. They rented two mules and began the descent into the canyon. Almost immediately, the bride's mule lost his footing and slipped. The woman said, "That's one." A short time later, he slipped once more. She said firmly, "That's two." After some time, the mule slipped yet again. The new bride was quite frustrated and said, "That's three." She promptly got off the mule, removed a thirty-eight revolver from her purse and shot the mule between the eyes. The horrified groom ran to the dead mule, glared at his wife and said, "What in the world did you do that for?" She frowned and said, "That's one." He told the reporter he never crossed her again. Forced compliance!

Life would be easier if we complied with God's purposes instead of being forced into the mold. We can fight His purpose or we can intentionally fit into His plan. God will complete what He has begun in us but our attitude is an important component in the process. How does this compliant attitude show itself in the real world?

We comply by refusing to argue.

> "The thing molded will not say to the molder, 'Why did you make me like this,' will it?" (Romans 9:20)

The obvious answer is, "No." However, we are often resistant to the difficult circumstances in our lives. We challenge Almighty God to answer our questions about why He is working in a particular manner. We are like spoiled children, with hands on hips, challenging our parent's authority. When we consistently question the sovereignty of God, the Potter has no choice but to crush us into a lump again.

Why do we continue to argue with His ways? We must learn to be compliant with the God of the universe since He has all knowledge and never makes a mistake. We see circumstances from a dimmed view but God sees clearly. We must trust His all-wise plan.

> "My thoughts are not your thoughts, neither are your ways My ways," declares the Lord. "For as the heavens are higher than the earth, so are My ways higher than your ways, and My thoughts than your thoughts." (Isaiah 55:9)

When we refuse to argue with God, even in difficult circumstances, we find deep joy. Someone told a woman who was suffering from a great hurt, "Suffering colors all of life, doesn't it?" She smiled and replied, "Yes, but I choose the color."

- What does God want you to do?
- What does God want you learn?
- Where does He want you to go?
- How much does He want you to give away?
- Do you find yourself arguing with the Lord about the way He is working in your life?
- Are you displeased with yourself and wish He had made you differently?

The potter has the authority to make from one lump of clay a beautiful vase or a water pot. Neither vessel has the right to argue with the maker. Which vessel would you rather be? In light of eternity, the water pot may be much more useful than the beautiful vase. Are you tempted to argue with God that He has not gifted you as He has others? Ann and I have a special friend named Alice Prince who was born with Down syndrome.

Alice finds it easy to share her love of Jesus with everyone she meets. She is a faithful prayer partner for our ministry. God has gifted her with an engaging smile and a warm heart. Her life is a constant witness for the Lord. Alice could argue with God about the way He made her; instead, her life is a testimony to God's grace and purpose. What an extraordinary person! Oh to have such a heart!

We comply with an attitude of acceptance.

We find a place of rest when we accept His design as best. Look at your life. Are you willing to bring your hurts, failures and burdens to God? In doing so, you will feel once again His loving hand upon you, remolding you to His will. God's way is perfect, regardless of the darkness that precedes the light. Acceptance of God's plan is not a mindset of futility. Rather, it is a faith glimpse of the future. God's character does not change and His purpose in molding always brings good.

"And we know that God causes all things to work together for good to those who love God, to those who are called according to His purpose." (Romans 8:28)

A potter can produce amazing results with ordinary clay. The Master Potter will work miracles in the lives of His children when we fully accept His sovereignty. God's love for us is certain. His intentions for us are honorable. His blessings can flow much more freely when our barrenness is accompanied with acceptance. The Great Giver will meet our needs in His way and in His time.

I return to the story of Jenise and Wade. When Luke came into their lives, they were so grateful for God's blessing. Their home was filled with the sounds of a baby. A well-organized house became a haven of bottles, blankets and bouncers. Life took on a new meaning. In retrospect, Jenise could see how compliance to God's will in her infertility had been rewarded.

When Luke was ten months old, Jenise received word from Luke's birth mother she was pregnant again. Jenise had the opportunity to adopt another baby. However, she immediately knew in her spirit this was not God's plan. Jenise told me, "Mom, I cannot take this baby when I know there are others in our church who desperately want a child. It would be selfish of me to take this baby when God has already given me one. I want another childless couple to have this blessing." I asked her to pray about it and God gave her this scripture, **"How good it is when brothers dwell together in unity." (Psalm 133:1)** Although this scripture seemed to indicate they should accept the baby, God continued to assure Jenise the baby was not to be hers. She determined the scripture meant Luke would know his brother through church. Another couple in our church was contacted and they wanted the baby. Jenise had been compliant to God's leading by allowing another couple to have their heart's desire fulfilled. This appeared to be the end of the story. However, God had another chapter to write.

Two months after the phone call from Luke's birth mother, Jenise discovered she was pregnant. This was truly a miracle of God! She was satisfied with the child God had given her and yet He had another promise to fulfill. Remember the scripture? **"The barren woman will abide in the house as a joyful mother of CHILDREN."** Through no help of modern medicine, she was pregnant. Due to her age and previous medical history, the doctors were concerned about the baby and her ability to carry it. However, the pregnancy went well; God had given Jenise the privilege of carrying a child. She said she never felt as beautiful as when she was pregnant. On Dec. 28, 2005, she gave birth to another son, Landon. He was the completion of God's promise, the long awaited fulfillment of scripture. He was beautiful, blond and blue-eyed. It was remarkable how much Landon looked like Luke. God planned for these two boys to be brothers and He did not miss a detail! The scripture God had given earlier was now clear. **"Behold, how good and how pleasant it is for brothers to dwell together in unity!" (Psalm 133:1)**

Again, I was asked to write a poem for Landon's birth announcement:

A CHRISTMAS MIRACLE

Trying to have a baby for several years,
  Only brought failure and many tears.
Some things medical science cannot do,
  But God's awesome power truly came through
Least expected was an addition to the fold,
  A second miracle for the Castle household.
God gave us a pregnancy though we were content,
  Now we have two sons, both heaven sent.
Join us in welcoming Luke's little brother,
  From a grateful Daddy and a joyful Mother.

God intended for Landon to be a part of the Castle family and his birth taught us much about God's providential love. God gave not only the couple at church a baby but also Jenise and Wade. When we look at Landon, we catch a glimpse of God's foreknowledge. God knew Jenise should not adopt another baby because she would soon be pregnant. What the doctors said could not be done, God did! Why do we ever doubt God's plan?

"With men this is impossible, but with God all things are possible." (Matthew 19:26b)

When we consider Landon's birth, we realize the timing was all-important. He was a special baby for a special time. If the three embryos had lived or Landon had been born first, we might never have had the blessing of Luke in our lives. Now we have two miracles and both are blessings beyond description.

I look up to heaven quite regularly and say, "Lord, you do know what you are doing. Despite our limited knowledge, You foresee. Despite our fears, You give us favor. Despite our faithlessness, You are faithful. Help me to be more compliant to Your will, because I have seen it is truly best."

Willing to Be Committed

For us to have the extraordinary life God desires for us, we must refuse to be conformed to the world's values. Instead, God requires that we be totally committed to Him. Such commitment will be demonstrated in a myriad of ways but the end result will be a life that glorifies God. *We cannot choose the specific labor of our commitment but we can choose the level of our commitment.* It is a contradiction to say we are partially committed. Our commitment to the Lord must be without reservation.

When Landon was born, he had great difficulty swallowing. In fact, for the first few months of his life, we had to force-feed him with a syringe. It was a time-consuming and difficult process. But when he became more developed, he could drink on his own. The time for force-feeding was over. The same is true with new Christians. God will protect the spiritually newborn soul. He will speak clearly and envelope that soul with Himself. But in time, God expects his child to develop a natural thirst and hunger for spiritual things. God will not continue to force-feed his children. He will not force you to a deeper level of commitment. It is your choice.

Commitment means having a thirst for God.

If we are to rise above the ordinary life, we must deeply desire more of God. We need to develop a real thirst for knowing God and search for the depths of Living Water continually.

"As the deer pants for the water brooks, so my soul pants for thee, O God. My soul thirsts for God, for the living God, when shall I come and appear before God?" (Psalm 42:1-2)

Water is a necessity of life. The normal human being can live only five days without water. None of us would want to go more than a day without drinking something to quench our thirst. Yet, often we become so distracted by the things of the world, our thirst for God is diminished. The truth is this: we may not be thirsty for God, but we suffer the effects of spiritual dehydration.

- How long can you live without a deep drink of God's Word?
- How long can you live without an intimate time in prayer with the God of the universe?
- How many months pass without your asking God for a refreshing breath of His Spirit?

Unfortunately, many Christians are content to sip at the fountain of God's reservoir. Thirst is the most basic of all appetites. *Only when we have a thirst for God, will the things of God be revealed.* God wants to break into our ordinary life and show us His supernatural power and Person. Are you willing to sacrifice the time necessary to daily drink from the Living Water through Bible study and prayer?

Commitment means being hungry for His will.

If we are to overcome the barrier of conformity to the world, we must allow the hunger for God's will to consume us, regardless of the cost. On a mission trip to the Philippines, our team stayed at a remote camp. The nationals traveled to the camp by foot, carrying bags of rice for the week's meals. Many walked for days to hear God's Word. Every meal for a week, the women cooked a blend of rice and water to make a thin soup. To add a small amount of taste to the soup, they confiscated discarded fish heads from the garbage of a market they passed on their way to the camp. Of course, it was extremely hot and I realized the fish heads had been without refrigeration for several days. Dying of food poisoning weighed heavily on my mind.

At first I merely tasted the soup and decided to subsist on my body fat. However, on the second day, the soup began to look more appetizing. By the third day, I decided rice, water and fish heads made a pretty good meal. One day, the fish head in my cup had a big, mushy eye and it was looking at me! A national woman became very excited and pointed at the fish eye. She began chanting something which being translated was, "Oh, she very lucky, she got fish eye. Very good for the stomach!" After seeing the fish eye, my stomach needed something else. Maybe Pepto Bismol?

They all gathered around to watch me dig out the fish eye, eat it and give my stomach good medicine. I dug it out, hid it in the bottom of the bowl, pretended to eat it, rubbed my stomach and smiled broadly. Thankfully, they weren't watching too closely; in time, my stomach settled down. I ate the soup for an entire week and it satisfied my hunger. However, my hunger had to become larger than my hang-ups about fish head soup, regardless of the cost.

By the same token, our hunger for God must become larger than our hang-ups concerning His will, regardless of the cost. How do we demonstrate we are hungry for His will?

- Be completely available to God.
- Totally trust God with our lives and our children's lives.
- Refuse to make excuses when He calls us to a task.
- Handle life's circumstances God's way.

Our lives should be marked with a commitment to live for Him, regardless of the circumstances, so that He will be glorified. My brother, Tommy Story, discovered recently he has lung cancer. Tommy is a "big time" farmer, tending hundreds of acres in West Tennessee. I was concerned about how he would handle this sickness after years of displaying physical strength and endurance. Much to my surprise, he handled it very well. Everywhere he went, he told people about the peace God had given him. It was not necessarily an assurance he would get well but that God would be with him each step of the way. He talked with the doctors about his assurance of heaven because of faith in Jesus Christ.

My brother's life has not been easy. He lost his wife, Janie, in a rafting accident twenty-eight years ago and was left a single father. He never lost his faith in a loving God, in spite of the questions concerning Janie's untimely death. God has blessed his life in many ways since that time. He eventually married a Christian lady and has watched his four children grow up.

Shortly before Tommy was to undergo surgery to remove part of his lung, a relative of Janie talked with him. This relative was a hardened unbeliever but had always loved Tommy. He searched for words as we often do when talking to someone who is facing a possible terminal illness. Finally he said, "Tommy, I hope you are going to be all right." Tommy just smiled and said, "I will be all right. Either I will survive this cancer or I will die and go to heaven. I will see Janie for the first time in twenty-eight years. I know where I am going because of my faith in Jesus Christ." Tears began to roll down the cheeks of this spiritually hardened man; he shook Tommy's hand and walked away. Tommy told me if his cancer had made this man think about his eternal home and the way to get there, then it was worth it. This is handling life's circumstances, God's way! I have much to learn from my big brother.

I also have much to learn from God about the insidious conformity that creeps into my life as a Christian. What about you? Are you ready to abandon the ordinary life of conformity and live as pliable clay in the hands of the Master Potter? If so, blessings await you beyond your wildest imaginations!

"For from old they have not heard nor perceived by the ear, neither has the eye seen a God besides Thee, Who acts in behalf of the one who waits for Him. But now, O Lord, Thou art our Father, we are the clay and thou our potter, and all of us are the work of Thy hand." (Isaiah 64: 4, 8)

Chapter 2

Fear Factor

"Do not fear, for I am with you; do not anxiously look about you, for I am your God. I will strengthen you, surely I will help you, surely I will uphold you with My righteous right hand." Isaiah 41:10

Section 1
The Paralysis of Fear

My chest had an invisible elephant standing on it; my breaths were shallow, stopping at my throat. Panic began to creep into my mind as I wrestled with the thought of fainting. As I sat in his chair, my hairdresser continued to make conversation while my thoughts raced, "Has he noticed I can't breathe? Should I ask him to call an ambulance? Am I dying?" Not wanting to pass out or call attention to myself, I continued to give short answers that would encourage him to talk without my participation. I began bargaining with God, "Lord, if you'll let me finish this haircut and leave, I promise to go to the emergency room."

It was 1990, the year my marriage unraveled, and I had noticed a marked shortness of breath when I ate. Ignoring the problem and the underlying stress that caused it, my health continued to deteriorate. Neglect and ignorance of my mental state finally brought me to a crisis point. Fiercely independent, I drove myself to the ER. (I do not recommend the reader try this.) Sure I was experiencing a heart attack, I was introduced to another malady-the panic attack. After an EKG and oxygen, the ER doctor asked if I was experiencing unusual stress. My words poured out more rapidly than my tears as I explained the problems in our home. He was the first of five doctors to recommend divorce in the weeks that followed.

During this time frame, I experienced fear in its most savage form, fear which stares you in the eyes when you wake in the morning and stands by the bed at night during fitful sleep. Panic attacks and shortness of breath continued during the subsequent months of separation and legal proceedings involving our family. However, I sensed in my spirit this was not God's way of handling a crisis. God understands man's fragile humanity, knowing fear is a major problem in daily life. I have not counted the phrase personally, but I've been told "Do not fear" appears in the Bible over three hundred times because God wants to reassure His fragile people. God gave me a life verse during this turmoil.

"Do not fear, for I am with you. Do not anxiously look about you, for I am your God. I will strengthen you, surely I will help you, surely I will uphold you with My righteous right hand." (Isaiah 41:10)

Fear is a major barrier to the extraordinary life of faith and adventure God calls Christians to live. Like young children, the unknown frightens us. We want to venture into the obedient life God is calling us to live, but logic and reason warn us to remain where it is familiar and safe. We fail to understand the safest place is found in obedience to the will of God. The most dangerous place to be is outside His plan and purpose. God calls His people to trust Him, not money, relationships or future plans.

I was a great planner during my teenage years and young adulthood. Being highly organized, I was able to control my environment to a great extent and placed my trust in self-made security. My marriage, church, community, in-laws, and friends were the blanket that covered my insecurities so I did not have to deal with fear. Once those things were wrestled from me, I was able to see my true Source of security since birth – The Father, who reveals Himself in Jesus Christ. My greatest lesson in life has been the discovery it is God who provides for me, regardless of whom is or is not in my life.

Universal Fear

Fear is a problem for both Christians and non-Christians who choose to live life the ordinary way. I recently visited the website for the National Non-Profit Mental Illness Advocacy Organization. Their statistics reveal at sometime during their lives, nearly a quarter (24.9%) of the adult population in the U.S. will have an anxiety disorder. The Anxiety Disorders Association website reveals similar, alarming statistics referring to the adult U.S. population. Their organization estimates 40 million of the adult U.S. population ages eighteen or older are affected by anxiety disorders at the present time.

- Generalized Anxiety Disorder – 6.8 million people or 3.1% of people
- Panic Disorders – 6 million, 2.7%
- Social Anxiety Disorder (excessive, persistent fear of social or performance situations) - 15 million, 6.8%
- Specific Phobia - 19 million, 8.7%

The statistics reveal women are twice as likely as men to experience generalized anxiety disorder, panic disorders, and specific phobias. Societal anxiety disorder is as common among men as women.

In addition to the mental toll of worry, anxiety disorders are a drain on our health care system. According to a study commissioned by the ADAA, anxiety disorders cost more than $42 billion a year, almost one third of the $148 billion total mental health bill for the U.S. The study reveals those with anxiety disorder are three to five times more likely to go to the doctor since many of the symptoms mimic physical illnesses.

"Do not fear," is wonderful advice but how do we accomplish fear-free living in this stressed out, burned out society in which we live? Terrorism, natural disasters such as hurricanes and tsunamis, sexual predators, family disintegration, crime and war are a few of the daily stress factors. Added to these are health problems, and the inevitable nature of death. Christians seem to be as burdened as the society surrounding them.

Carolyn and I taught a study on freedom from fear several Wednesday nights at our church. The ladies' group we were leading tripled in size when we announced the topic. The second week of our study, we asked the women to record their fears. We were shocked as a list was compiled that filled two pages, typed and single-spaced. I want to share some of what was listed:

- Fear of death or death of a child
- Not having enough money
- Weight getting out of control
- Losing my job
- Something tragic happening to my family
- Fear of rejection when giving my testimony
- Fear of the future
- Fear I will not please my husband or boss

The most heart-wrenching statement I read was this: fear my children will someday not love me. Remember, this list was from a group of Christians and church members committed enough to be at church on Wednesday night.

Causes of Fear

How can we balance our humanity with the supernatural life, free of worry and anxiety? We need to examine the causes of fear and the responses we make to them. Once we are educated on the triggers of fear, we can begin to mature beyond them. I read a shark will not grow beyond the boundaries of his environment. There are perfectly formed and mature sharks that are only six inches long because they have been left in an aquarium. If removed from the aquarium and placed in the ocean, the same sharks will grow to several feet. In the same way, fear limits our development as a Christian by keeping our focus on the problems of life rather than the vastness of God's plan and will. There are two causes of fear we need to examine: situational fear and sin.

Situational Fear

The first trigger for fear is found in negative or adverse circumstances. I call this *situational fear*. Granted, many of life's circumstances appear frightening. I do not want to be insensitive to people who have experienced great tragedy in life which has left them vulnerable and anxious. The good news of the Bible is we do not have to experience fear as the world does, regardless of our circumstances. Isaiah 8:12-13, directs our fear away from situations and toward the only object in life worthy of our fear, God.

"You are not to say, 'It is a conspiracy!' in regard to all that this people call a conspiracy, and you are not to fear what they fear or be in dread of it. It is the Lord of hosts whom you should regard as holy, and He shall be your fear, and He shall be your dread."

Death. Fear of a Sovereign God is nothing like the quaking fear we exhibit when confronted with adversity. Fear of God means reverence and awe of Who He is: *all-powerful* and always *present* with us. It has been said all human fear is rooted in the fear of death. God has promised His *presence* with us in the shadow of death and He has also promised His Sovereignty has overcome death's *power*.

"Even though I walk through the valley of the shadow of death, I fear no evil, for You are with me; Your rod and Your staff, they comfort me." (Psalm 23:4)

"Death is swallowed up in victory. O death where is your victory? O death where is your sting?" (I Corinthians 15:54c-55)

"And He placed His right hand on me, saying, 'Do not be afraid; I am the first and the last, and the living One; and I was dead, and behold, I am alive forevermore, and I have the keys of death and of Hades.'" (Revelations 1:17b-18)

If God's presence and power have defeated our ultimate enemy, death, then daily problems can be lived in victory if we place our trust in Him. I have a calendar with a quotation by Elizabeth Elliot for every day of the year. Elizabeth was married to Jim Elliot, a missionary slain in South America by the tribe he was trying to reach with the Gospel. She writes on

June 12, "The love of God has wrapped us round from before the foundation of the world. If we fear him–that is, if we reverence and worship Him in absolute assurance of His Sovereignty–we cannot possibly be afraid of anything else. To love God is to destroy all other fear." Be comforted, the Heavenly Father is the solution to your fears. He is bigger than your fears and able to overcome the punishment that accompanies them.

Panic attacks and phobias. What about panic attacks? There was no enemy in the room when I experienced the symptoms that drove me to seek medical attention. Panic attacks are nature's response to a threat; therefore, our ability to use God's perspective on our problems eliminates the perception of threat. Phobias are also irrational fears based upon misconception. As a child I experienced a phobia about germs. Once I realized invisible, microscopic bacteria roamed around, I washed my hands dozens of times a day. In fact, I would run into the house from playing in the dirt, wash my hands, grab the doorknob with my wrists to open the outside door, and proceed directly back to play in the dirt! Most of our phobia responses make the same kind of sense.

As an adult, I experienced a new phobia-an aversion to being the center of attention. Even today when I walk in a room, I keep a low profile to prevent people from looking directly at me. Only God's grace enables me to teach the Bible or lead a conference before a group. Occasionally, extreme confidence in my personal appearance allows me joy at being noticed. One year Carolyn and I had a series of denominational meetings over a two-day period. I made an effort to coordinate my clothing so I would need only one pair of dress shoes. The first day, I wore black dress shoes and knee-high stockings with my dark pantsuit. The next day, we had a meeting that required a skirt, so I packed black pantyhose to wear with the same shoes. I had a new dress coat that was gray with black velvet trim, and I was elated to be completely color coordinated.

The second morning we were running late, so I jumped into my pantyhose, quickly dressed in my black suit and coat, grabbed the handle of my wheeled suitcase, and slipped into my shoes on the way out the door. Carolyn was ahead of me as we emerged from the elevator of the upscale hotel where we were staying. She quickly walked to get the car. As I started across the lobby, I noticed everyone was looking at me. Confident their stares were due to my perfectly coordinated wardrobe, I allowed myself a few seconds of joy at my effort to look attractive. Joy quickly turned to horror when I looked down at my shoes. In my haste, I failed to notice my knee-high stockings had been thrown on top of my shoes the night before. As I slipped my feet into the shoes, the sideways knee-highs hung out both sides of each shoe and were dusting the hardwood floor as I walked.

No one enjoys a good laugh more than Carolyn, but I was not in the mood to allow her one so early in the morning at my expense. I planned to reach down quickly, grab the knee-highs, and stuff them in my coat pocket before she saw my dilemma. Just as I reached for the second stocking, Carolyn turned around and started laughing so hard she bent double. Suddenly my phobia at being noticed roared back as *everyone* in the lobby began to chuckle. Before I could feel afraid, I realized how funny I looked and joined in the humor of the moment. When afflicted with a phobia, the ability to laugh helps tremendously!

The best way to handle a phobia is to realize there is no factual basis to support the response to an anxiety-producing situation. I saw an acrostic for fear that sums up its basis.

> F – false
> E – evidence
> A – appearing
> R – real

Absolute trust in the goodness of God will overcome *situational fear* and allow us to lead a supernatural life unfettered by the chains of anxiety and worry. The Truth of Christ will cancel false evidence if we seek His perspective on problems. I am not an expert in psychology, but I am a fellow sufferer who has experienced both ragged fear and the reality of the loving care of the Good Shepherd. *Situational fear is a trust issue.*

Another sufferer was the prophet Elijah. In I Kings, Elijah experienced two miracles from God in chapter 18-fire from heaven that consumed his water-soaked sacrifice on Mt. Carmel and the rainstorm that came after three and a half years of drought.

"Then the fire of the Lord fell and consumed the burnt offering and the wood and stones and the dust, and licked up the water that was in the trench. When all the people saw it, they fell on their faces; and they said, 'The Lord, He is God; the Lord, He is God.' Then Elijah said to them, 'Seize the prophets of Baal; do not let one of them escape.' So they seized them; and Elijah brought them down to the brook Kishon, and slew them there." (I Kings 18:38-40)

"In a little while the sky grew black with clouds and wind, and there was a heavy shower. And Ahab rode and went to Jezreel. Then the hands of the Lord was on Elijah, and he girded up his loins and outran Ahab to Jezreel." (I Kings:18:45-46)

Elijah was a brave prophet and a valiant prayer warrior, who killed 450 prophets of Baal, proving God was the one true God. On the heels of this great victory, despair overcame Elijah when an enraged Jezebel threatened his life. I Kings 19:3, outlines Elijah response, **"And he was afraid and arose and ran for his life..."** Elijah had a *situation* and he responded with fear. Imagine how ridiculous it was that he had slain the prophets of Baal but was fleeing at the threats of a woman. Where was the God who had sent flames down to the altar in I Kings 18:38? God was still *present* with Elijah and was as *powerful* as He had been the previous day on Mt. Carmel. Elijah failed to acknowledge Him or seek His leadership, the same mistakes we make when gripped by fear. We quickly forget past blessings of God when we encounter a new enemy. As Christians, we need long memories of God's goodness and sharp ears to listen to His directions.

Years ago I taught a Sunday school class in my church. I tried to pray before each lesson and be open to new insights God might allow me to share. One Sunday I was excited with the spiritual truths revealed from Scripture, and I prayed before I left home that morning, "Oh, Lord, if I could give these insights to the women, I would pay them twenty dollars each to listen and let the truth sink into their hearts." God immediately impressed into my spirit His answer, "Ann, I've paid them hundreds of thousands of dollars over years and years, and they still will not listen to Me." I was stunned; we all need to be stunned that the God of the universe is speaking to us daily, and we are too distracted to listen. His direction could lead us through or around situations that produce anxiety.

Finances. Some of the most frightening times I experienced as a single parent were financial. In the middle of the night, my eyes would pop open and my brain would engage its calculator. The figures did not add up to stretch salary and child support over the monthly bills. Yet, I can share with you the faithfulness of God through my children's years at home. I never missed paying a bill on time, buying groceries, clothing, gasoline or any other necessity. At times I had to explain to my children there were activities or items we could not afford, which is not harmful to children. They learned to practice budgeting of allowances and stretching money by searching for bargains.

I promised myself not to forget one experience. When I received our rental property as my part of the financial settlement, I also received the mortgage attached to it. The first mortgage check I wrote, I was shaking so badly I had to get in bed and turn on the electric blanket. I have not missed a mortgage payment in fifteen years, again proving God's faithfulness.

I continued to tithe, sometimes cashing my child support check and physically taking the tithe to the church office. I explained to our secretary several times, "If I don't bring this to you now, it will be gone." Our needs were great, but God was greater.

I had a pattern in my life of giving to the mission's offerings our denomination collects annually. One year in the midst of financial reversals, there was no money to give to the spring offering. I remember crying and explaining to God (as if He did not know) my financial situation. I promised in my prayer if anything unexpected found its way to my bank account I would use it for the offering. Several days later a couple close to Carolyn asked it I needed anything. Carolyn shared how tight my finances were and they gave me $300.00. That gift became my spring offering and was more than I had been able to give in years past. I was elated and encouraged by God's abundant response. He provided as I went to Him in prayer, asking, expecting, and listening.

Sin

The second trigger for fear in our lives is *sin*. Yes, lack of trust in the *presence* and *power* of our Savior, failure to listen and acknowledge His leadership is a *sin* problem. It is *sin* to seek for solutions out of human wisdom when confronted by frightening situations. Elijah prayed earnestly in I Kings, chapter 18, and he experienced miracles of God. In chapter 19, receiving the bad news of Jezebel's threat, Elijah fails to pray. He relied upon conventional wisdom, packed his bags, and left town as quickly as possible. How many times are we weighing our options when we should be praying? Often, we are on the phone when we should be on our knees, reading the bank statement when we should be reading the Bible.

During the property settlement connected with our divorce, I made copies of the legal papers. Carolyn and I prayed over them at length, and then burned them. I wanted to demonstrate in a tangible way my belief that God, not attorneys, judges, nor courts, would have the final word in my life. I encourage those of you dealing with fearful situations to pray and then take action to show God your faith in His goodness and His Word. To hide, cry, and shake when confronted by adversity is *sin*, and I have been guilty at times. I compare the fear barrier in life to a wall that suddenly appears. We have a choice as to our reaction. We can lie down in front of the wall, weep, and tell all who will listen how high and insurmountable the wall is. We can go to sleep, resting on the wall, becoming familiar and comfortable with our pain, hoping someone else will rescue us. Or we can find a way to scale the wall, get around it, or dig through it. The Way is found through our faith in Jesus Christ. Taking tangible action is not relying upon works. It is showing our Father and those around us *by* our works we have faith in Him.

Elijah was a great man of God. How could he have allowed the sin of distrust to take hold of his decision-making process? Sin is insidious and progressive. It clogs our relationship to our Savior, rendering us incapable of hearing His directions. Carolyn and I try to meet every morning we can to exercise. We walk at a park near our homes on a wilderness trail with challenging hills and beautiful scenery. Recently as we were walking, we encountered an Asian woman who was walking backwards. While I'm sure walking backwards has health benefits in utilizing different muscles, this woman was constantly looking over her shoulder to keep her bearings. When we fail to acknowledge God's trustworthiness we are walking backwards. We must constantly look over our shoulder to see if the object of our fear is approaching.

Sin is also accompanied by *guilt*, and guilt carries punishment. Many people I have counseled are wracked with the guilt of sin that has been confessed and already forgiven by God. People's memories work against them when their focus becomes the past transgression rather than the mercy of God. If you are riddled by guilt from past sin, ask the Father to forgive you now. If He directs you to make restitution to someone, immediately obey. If He has already forgiven you, then rest in His mercy and focus your attention on the future.

The Downward Spiral

In its progressive nature, sin leads to the third cause of fear, the downward *spiral*. The fear *spiral* is a dangerous possibility for those who fail to deal with threatening situations God's way. Elijah's flight from Jezebel was not the end of his fear cycle, only the beginning. Flight led to depression as Elijah surrenders to defeat and requests God to take his life.

"But he himself went a day's journey into the wilderness, and came and sat down under a juniper tree; and he requested for himself that he might die, and said, 'It is enough; now, O Lord, take my life, for I am not better than my fathers.'" (I Kings 19:4)

The scripture strongly implies Elijah was not eating, only sleeping. Self-pity gives way to depression, which can lead to physical harm, even suicide.

While depression is anger turned inward, many people become outwardly angry with God when facing fearful situations. Anger toward God is as useless as a child boxing the wind. I recently babysat with Skylar, my five-year-old granddaughter. We had a good time playing various games while my daughter was at work. Late in the afternoon I encouraged Skylar to begin picking up her toys. This darling child who had been a bundle of enthusiasm and energy all day suddenly was too tired to pick up even one toy. She kept nagging me to help her. I cleaned up half the toys since I had been playing with her, but I refused to complete the job, knowing she needed training in responsibility. After several requests, she wrinkled her nose, put her hands on her hips and said, "Can't you see how mad I am?" Stifling a laugh, I assured her that her anger made no difference. She still needed to clean up her toys. In the same manner, our anger with God has no effect upon His plans and purposes. He simply waits for us to accept His direction for our life. If we fail to acknowledge Him, anger inevitably turns to bitterness and withdrawal.

I own rental property in a nearby county. Because I live out of town, I am dependent on my employees to report problems. One night, my manager called to say we had a big problem, "When the toilet in apartment 7 is flushed, the sewage comes up in the bathtub of apartment 8." A real problem! There were three apartments completely stopped up as the pipe was blocked with sewage. The building is old with aging sewer lines, and the blockage had been building for years. Suddenly, nothing was moving. Fear works the same way, one anxiety at a time slowly clogging the flow of God's Spirit until the downward spiral requires His intervention.

We climbed on the roof the next day and the maintenance man ran a tape down the vent and continued to push the sewage through the pipe. We descended to the basement and opened the clean-out valve. I cannot begin to describe (and you would not want me to) the smell and filth that flowed into the basement. The conclusion of the fear spiral is the exposure of the negativity that began with unchecked worry and anxiety and concludes with anger, distrust, isolation, and bitterness. When you are surprised by your reaction to an adverse situation, remember that what is inside is what comes to the surface. The harboring of resentment, fear, and bitterness will eventually conclude with a "blow" of stinking emotions at a crisis point.

Will you choose today to step out and begin to walk the fear-free life of an obedient Christian? Reversals are the time we clearly see the loving hand of the Father if we react with trust rather than anxiety. Focusing our attention on Christ, rather than circumstances, allows us to navigate by a point that never changes. Gazing on our problems, rather than on Him, produces hesitation, disobedience and harm in life.

Years ago, my father worked for a large insurance company that required its agents go door to door to collect premiums. One day a month, Dad went into the rural area surrounding our Alabama community. He shared one particular house had a large dog that had always lain on the front porch. Usually, the dog was asleep or lounging lazily when he arrived, and he would step over him to reach the front door. One day the dog was in the yard as my father came around the house. He was surprised to see the pet awake and walking. He fixed his gaze on the animal and registered fear.

The big dog immediately lunged for him. Dad was wearing a wristwatch that prevented a bite on his left arm. The animal continued to bite at him, locking on to his briefcase next. Thoroughly frightened by this time, Dad ran back to his car, closed his door and waited.

The dog began to stalk, proceeded to the back bumper, grabbed it with his teeth and shook the car. My amazed father then saw the animal approach the front driver's side tire, sink his teeth into it, and flatten the tire! Dad dared not attempt to change it at that location, but drove the car to a neighbor's house. He says the tire was beyond repair and had to be replaced. The problem began when my father fixed his gaze on the dog and registered fear.

Similarly, when we fix our gaze on the adversities of life, rather than on the saving power of Jesus Christ, we open ourselves to the ravages of fear. God asks us to center our thoughts on Him, trust His care, and heed His Word.

"Finally, brethren, whatever is true, whatever is honorable, whatever is right, whatever is pure, whatever is lovely, whatever is of good repute, if there is any excellence and if anything worthy of praise, dwell on these things." (Philippians 4:8)

A life centered on Christ is the life poised to step onto the path of faith and extraordinary living. You have the power to choose faith over fear.

Section 2

Faith the Solution

In January of 2005, I began to notice my eyesight was failing. However, it was not the normal condition where eyesight dims with age. Objects suddenly began to look wavy and would actually disappear at certain angles. Because of a planned mission trip to New York City, I postponed going to the optometrist. When I returned, I heard the discouraging diagnosis of macular degeneration.

I was referred to a specialist, and he concluded it was not macular degeneration but actually a hole in the macula. This condition is quite rare and often results in blindness. However, with recent developments in technology, surgery was possible. I discovered the recuperation time was far more difficult than the surgery. The operation took place in Nashville on February 14, a real gift for Valentine's Day. Following the surgery, I had to lie on my stomach on a board with a hole cut out for my face for ten days; looking at the floor at all times. I ached in joints I did not know were in my body. At the same time, I was grateful for modern medicine and the promise of renewed eyesight.

Six weeks after the surgery, Ann and I were scheduled to be in California for the wedding of a good friend, Cathleen Sward. (We met Cathleen as the other member of our mission team that traveled to Iran.) Although the wedding was in Fresno, we had to fly into the San Francisco airport. I was somewhat fearful about driving in this city due to horror stories about the freeways and terrible traffic. (Considering my handicap, you may question why Ann did not drive on this particular trip. The answer is simple: She hates to drive.) The doctor cleared me to go and after much prayer, we felt God's leadership to attend the wedding.

We arrived at the airport, rented a car, and left the city before rush hour. God was with us, directed every turn, and we drove to Fresno without incident. The wedding was beautiful and we were able to renew fellowship with Cathleen and meet her new husband.

On our way back to San Francisco, we drove into a thunderstorm. We were both praying the storm would diminish before we returned to the city. Yet, as providence would have it, the storm became worse. Approaching San Francisco, I saw a maze of interstates, all merging at the same place. To accomplish this maze, some crazed engineer had drawn plans for certain interstates to spiral upward, rise above the others, merge with specific freeways and eventually return to ground level. Since the traffic flow set the speed, I had to drive at a similar speed-FAST. Ann and I found ourselves speeding up a steep spiral, in the rain, and having no clear idea of where to merge when we reached the top.

As we reached the peak, Ann said, "It is raining really hard," to which I replied, "I know." Then she said, "We are going really fast," to which I replied, "I know." Finally she said in a quaking voice, "We are really, really high in the sky," to which I replied, "I know." She then buried her head in her hands and said, "And YOU are Blind Tom!" Trying to keep my cool, I said in as controlled a voice as I could muster, "Well, I don't know which has less sense, Blind Tom driving or the one who is riding with Blind Tom!" We survived our trek to California but we doubted our sanity for making such a journey with one eye!

Faith's Pilgrimage

I recounted the trip as an illustration concerning fear. We all develop fears concerning certain things or situations. Fear is something that chips away at the very core of our being. We have to place our fears in God's hands and proceed with life's experiences as He leads. *We have a haven where fear has no place of habitation.* This haven is discovered through total faith in God. Whatever the circumstance, we can rest in the assurance He will not fail us.

"The Lord is the one who goes ahead of you; He will be with you. He will not fail you or forsake you. Do not fear or be dismayed." (Deuteronomy 31:8)

The Bible repeats often the admonition, "Do not fear." God, knowing our weaknesses, has to give us remedial courses in Do Not Fear 101. As we overcome fear and worry, we begin to experience the extraordinary life God intends for His children.

- We *mentally* find *stability* when we acknowledge His sovereignty in all situations.
- We s*piritually* experience *peace* to the depths of our soul.
- We *physically* retain *strength* with a life virtually free of worry and fear.
- We *emotionally* find *security* in His power.

Physicians tell us fear and worry are the major causes of the majority of hospital stays in America. Fear results in worry; worry results in stress; stress results in sickness. God, the Creator, knew it would be harmful to His children's health to worry and fret. Therefore, He reminds us consistently to put aside our concerns and trust Him with everything. Since it is obvious by reading God's Word we are not to be fearful or worry, how can we accomplish the goal of stress-free living?

We must first be certain we have a personal, intimate relationship with God through faith in Jesus Christ. We can meet life's difficult times with the assurance and knowledge our Heavenly Father is in control. He loves us more than we can imagine and He is fully aware of the events taking place in our world.

We need to meditate on the power and strength of God, rather than concentrating on our difficulty. When we compare our problems with the power of Almighty God, the problems dwindle in size. In Biblical times, Jehoshaphat was facing a mighty army and was greatly afraid. He went to the Lord in prayer.

"We are powerless before this great multitude who are coming against us; nor do we know what to do, but our eyes are on Thee." (II Chronicles 20:12)

God responds, **"Do not fear or be dismayed because of this great multitude, for the battle is not yours but God's." (II Chronicles 20:15)**

We have the same assurance from the Lord. The battle is not ours to win if we allow God to intervene on our behalf. We must learn to look beyond the problem to God's promise:

"For momentary, light affliction is producing for us an eternal weight of glory far beyond all comparison, while we look not at the things which are seen, but at the things which are not seen; for the things which are seen are temporal, but the things which are not seen are eternal." (II Corinthians 4:17-18)

Faith's Possibilities

Are you secure in God's ability to take care of your problem? I am reminded of a time my granddaughter, Olivia, visited me. A few days earlier, I had purchased digital bathroom scales. Noticing the new scales, she jumped on them and she weighed 29 pounds. Olivia was born prematurely and has always been small. I tried to explain weight to her and she asked me to weigh. I weighed 129 pounds. I laughed and said, "Olivia, La La weighs exactly 100 pounds more than you do." Her eyes grew large and she looked scared. I asked what was wrong and she said, "La La, if something happens to you, I can't carry you very far."

The wonderful thing for us to consider is that God can carry us as far as we need to be carried. His power is unlimited. When we are exhausted from the weight of our problems, God is able to execute a wealth of power on our behalf. When we can go no farther, we must trust the Father.

"For the Lord will vindicate His people and will have compassion on His servants; when He sees that their strength is gone." (Deuteronomy 32:36)

Hattie Green is known as the world's most famous miser. She died in 1918, leaving an estate of over 100 million dollars. Yet she lived like a pauper. She had only one son who was the apple of her eye. She and her son subsisted on oatmeal, which she refused to cook because it would cost too much to heat. As a young child, the son developed an infection in his leg. Rather than hire a taxi to take him to a free medical clinic, Hattie Green chose to stay at home and take care of him. Eventually the son's leg had to be amputated and he died from the infection. Hattie Green lived several more years but died from malnutrition. In reality, she had an abundance of resources but failed to use them. What about you?

- Do you live as a spiritual pauper, failing to use all the resources of power God has at your disposal?
- Do you find yourself worrying about situations and failing to see God has promised to meet your every need according to His riches?
- Are you content to live as a spiritual pauper, trying to plan the next step, handling life as best you can, and worrying excessively along the way?
- Are you weary of fear consuming your focus and energy?

Worry can even become a badge of honor, which we wear and talk about often to our friends. Mothers boast about how much they worry over their children as if the more they worry, the better parent they are. This is totally unscriptural and not pleasing to God. Worry is diametrically opposed to faith. Either we have faith and do not worry or we worry and do not have faith. How do we come to the place where anxiety, worry and stress are replaced with faith?

Faith's Position

Imagine yourself attending a conference with a large audience. There are two chairs on the stage placed about eight inches apart. On one of the chairs is a sign "Total Trust in God" and on the other chair a sign "Worldly Ways." The speaker asks you to come to the stage and sit in either of the chairs for the remainder of the conference. You would probably be hesitant but might comply at his insistence. However, what if he asked you to sit on part of one chair and part of the other chair-with nothing in the middle? You would probably refuse. Why? It is because you might fall and be embarrassed or at least, you would be uncomfortable.

Regrettably, this is where most Christians sit spiritually. When they became a Christian, they totally trusted God for salvation. They left the "chair" of the world and became a part of God's Kingdom by moving into the "chair" of trust. However somewhere in life, they slipped out of the position of total trust. They did not move entirely into worldly ways but stopped somewhere in the middle. It is a place that is uncomfortable, lacks God's peace, and becomes a place of worry. They are saved but not allowing God full control over their lives and circumstances.

If we are to overcome the barrier of fear, we must realize God knows what is best for our children and us. When we cannot see the light at the end of the tunnel, God states the light is there nonetheless. We must trust Him to bring us to the light.

Many years ago in Kentucky, two young spelunkers decided to explore an undeveloped cave system that ran underneath the entire area. Knowing little about cave exploration, they soon became lost. In complete darkness, they began to cry out for help but no one could hear. As nighttime approached, the parents became concerned and began asking questions around town. They learned the boys had entered the cave but had not been heard from since. The distraught parents called for help in finding their sons.

Several would-be rescuers searched for the boys for three days but the spelunkers had gone too far into the cave. The parents were told it would be impossible to find them since there were numerous tunnels and rivers in the cavern. In desperation, one of the fathers requested the help of an elderly man whose home was over the cave. This old farmer had bragged about playing in the cave as a child and he continued to explore the cave throughout his life. He knew the hidden tunnels and agreed to search for the boys.

For several agonizing hours, the parents waited and prayed. Finally, two scared, hungry young men crawled out of the cave, followed by the old farmer. The reason for the old man's success was his complete knowledge of the cave. He had been there before. He could sit in his home and mentally picture the interior of the cavern. He knew far more about the cave than anyone, which is why he was asked to help, even though a rescue seemed hopeless.

Often we find ourselves in situations that seem hopeless. Our children come to us hurting and in despair. What do we do?

- Do we sit and worry?
- Do we spend our time telephoning family and friends?
- Do we plot ways we can make things right?
- Do we attempt to predict the outcome?
- Do we seek help from the One who has been there before?

God sees the entire world, He knows the way out of the problem. He is the Great Guide. He is willing to lead His children to safety if we allow Him.

"For Thou art my rock and my fortress; for Thy name's sake Thou wilt lead me and guide me." (Psalm 31:3)

God desires to guide you out of the pit of worry. He would like to see you go through the barrier of fear into the blessings of the faith life. He will lead you step by step as you walk in obedience to His voice. These steps are outlined in the following scripture:

"On the third day there was a wedding in Cana of Galilee, and the mother of Jesus was there; and both Jesus and His disciples were invited to the wedding. When the wine ran out, the mother of Jesus said to Him, 'They have no wine.' And Jesus said to her, 'Woman, what does that have to do with us? My hour has not yet come.' His mother said to the servants, 'Whatever He says to you, do it.' Now there were six stone waterpots set there for the Jewish custom of purification, containing twenty or thirty gallons each. Jesus said to them, 'Fill the waterpots with water.' So they filled them up to the brim. And He said to them, 'Draw some out now and take it to the headwaiter.' So they took it to him. When the headwaiter tasted the water which had become

wine, and did not know where it came from (but the servants who had drawn the water knew), the headwaiter called the bridegroom, and said to him, 'Every man serves the good wine first, and when the people have drunk freely, then he serves the poorer wine, but you have kept the good wine until now.'" (John 2:1-10)

Step 1: Prayer

When the wedding party ran out of wine, Mary went immediately to Jesus and said, "We have no wine." She did not feel it necessary to give a long explanation of the circumstances or cause of this embarrassing situation. Neither did she give Him an agenda of how He should work. She approached Jesus, stated the problem and trusted Him with the solution.

We need to be in constant communication with the Lord. When we have a concern, we simply need to approach Jesus, state the problem and, like Mary, trust Him to do what is best. He is our Source. Our prayers need to be specific and direct. God knows our problem before we come to him but we need to acknowledge clearly our desire.

"Let us therefore draw near with confidence to the throne of grace, that we may receive mercy and find grace to help in time of need." (Hebrews 4:16)

Some time ago, Ann and I had a conference in Birmingham, Alabama. We checked into a motel and found the only bath linens in the room were towels and hand towels. I leaned into the hallway and asked the housekeeper for two bath cloths. She seemed confused and looked at the other worker with a questioningly look. She asked, "You want what?" "I want two bath cloths; we have towels and hand towels but no bath cloths." I replied. She was getting really frustrated with me and asked again, "Now what in the world do you say you want?" Ann, being from Alabama, stuck her head out and said, "She wants WARSH RAGS." The vindicated housekeeper replied, "Well, why didn't she say that then?" Somehow, I had not made myself clear. However, God has no problem understanding our cry for help.

Many times we are like the Pharisee who prayed and thought he would be heard for his many words. We concern ourselves with the method of prayer, attempting to say the right words, in the right form, so we will get the right result. God wants us to simply state our needs and leave the filling of those needs up to Him. Simplicity is clear to His understanding ear.

"I sought the Lord and He answered me, and delivered me from all my fears." (Psalm 34:4)

Step 2: Penitence

When Mary came to Jesus with her requests, there was nothing in their relationship that prevented her from approaching him. We must come to God with clean hearts. We need to be honest with ourselves concerning our sins and confess them. Sin separates us from fellowship with the Father but repentance renews the fellowship. Resolve any spiritual conflicts you have with your Father and other people. You may need to:

- Confess you are not totally dependant upon God and feel defeated.
- Ask God's forgiveness for worrying when you should be worshipping.
- Refrain from spreading bad news instead of sharing the Good News.
- Extend forgiveness instead of nursing anger.
- Place God first instead of last on your "to do" list.
- Be willing to allow God's light to search your life for things that are not pleasing to Him.
- Examine the reasons for your lack of spiritual growth.
- Seek God's cleansing in every area of your life that is not holy.

"If we confess our sins, He is faithful and righteous to forgive us our sins and to cleanse us from all unrighteousness." (I John 1:9)

Step 3: Partition

We must separate the facts from the "what ifs." When my son, Jeff, was five years old, we visited my in-laws over Easter weekend. As we left for church, Jeff saw a bowl of mints on the table. He asked for one but I denied him the privilege, knowing he would get candy on his hands and new suit. Although I was not aware of it, Jeff asked his grandmother for a mint. Of course, she gave it to him. We arrived at the church and filled the pew with our children and my husband's family.

Jeff was at the age when his front teeth were getting loose. He would grin and wiggle the loose teeth with his tongue and I would shudder. Sometime during the service, Jeff took the mint out of his mouth and was holding it in his hand; by this time, it was only a sliver. I looked down, saw the white sliver and asked him what it was. He whispered, "It's my tooth." I, in turn, whispered to my husband, "Jeff pulled his tooth." Like the speed of light, the word traveled across the pew to the members of the family. At this point, I began to worry. *What if* his gums began to bleed? Worse yet, *what if* he got blood on his new suit?

Suddenly, he put the sliver back in his mouth and began to crunch it. I whirled to my husband, shuddered and said, "Jeff ate his tooth!" All the people on the pew heard the commotion and asked what had happened. The word filtered throughout the family that Jeff had eaten his tooth. Everyone began to shudder as he continued to crunch. Realizing he had the entire pew at his command, he made strange faces and chewed the "tooth" with all his might.

I began to have new concerns. *What if* he broke another tooth chewing on the pulled one? *What if* he choked on his tooth? *What if* it made him sick? To be honest, I had never heard of a child eating a tooth. Now mine had done just that!

I turned Jeff toward me, ready to give him CPR. He flashed a wide smile, wiggled his teeth and said it was just a mint he had eaten. I would have killed him if I had not been so busy trying to muffle my laughter. I had worried about the "what ifs" but none happened. I should have stuck with the facts.

Mary was not concerned with the "what ifs" when the wedding party exhausted their supply of wine. However, this was a crucial time for the family of a Jewish couple due to the emphasis on celebrations for weddings. The wedding lasted a week and everyone was invited. Wine and food were expected to be in abundance. When the lack of wine was discovered, Mary went to Jesus and stated, "We have no wine." She did not say, "*What if* this family is going to be the laughing stock of the town?" "*What if* no one ever visits here again?" She stated the facts and did not dwell on what the future might hold.

Several years ago my husband, Danny, was hired by a company, which was well known as a leader in banking service and equipment. He was a trained service technician in that field and was eager to join this 150-year-old company. They were known as the grandfather of the banking service industry. The retirement plan for the firm consisted of investing in company stocks, which was matched by the employer. We sacrificed and saved as much as we could each year in preparation for retirement. One day my husband called and said the company had declared bankruptcy and was closing. The CEO had liquidated all the funds and fled to Germany. In one second, our seemingly secure retirement became non-existent. My mind began to race with "what ifs."

- *What if* we lose the house?
- *What if* we cannot get health insurance?

- *What if* we never find another job?
- *What if* we starve to death?

The longer I thought about the situation, the more fear consumed my heart and mind. I began to pray and almost immediately God reminded me of a scripture.

"And my God shall supply all your needs according to His riches in glory in Christ Jesus." (Philippians 4:19)

God spoke in my spirit and asked if I believed His Word. I responded in faith by believing His promises. I determined not to worry about anything but to trust God's provisions. A peace came over me like a warm blanket. The peace remained until 2:00 in the morning when I awoke in a panic; the "what ifs" were back. Again, God whispered, "Do you believe me?" From that moment, I refused to worry about the "what ifs." I stated the facts in prayer and God continued to provide for our family. In due time, my husband was employed by a smaller company and continues to work there. We did not lose our home, we have health insurance and we certainly did not starve to death. In fact, it seems we continue to gain weight!

If we had lost our home, would it have mattered in light of eternity? No! Nothing is sacred about living in a particular house. Examine your worry list. Ask yourself if these problems have eternal significance. Determine if the things on your worry list are actual facts or if they fall into the "what if" category of fear. *If the fears are not facts, dismiss them.*

"Through presumption comes nothing but strife." (Proverbs 13:10a)

Step 4: Participate

Mary told the servants to do whatever Jesus told them. They filled the pots to the brim with water. The servants did exactly what Jesus said. They completed the action Jesus required for His miracle. Jesus worked the miracle but He used the servants in the process.

God wants to work a miracle in your life by delivering you from fear and worry. However, you may have a responsibility to fulfill in the miracle. God will call you to action to defeat the fear that hinders your life. The best way to overcome fear is to face it and do the thing you fear the most, with the help of the Holy Spirit. Trust God to perform the miracle in you just as completely as He did with the empty water pots at the wedding. He will respond when you totally trust Him in faith. *The key is God's power, not our performance.*

I was painfully shy as a child. Although I was born into a wonderful Christian home, I found it impossible to make conversation during family meals. My fear of people made it difficult to make new friends and I was quite a loner. Unfortunately, my shyness did not disappear as I grew older and it made me miserable. I was filled with fear each time I was asked to read aloud in school or quote a scripture verse at church. Social gatherings brought a special uncomfortable situation and I shunned them whenever possible.

As a teenager, I determined to overcome my fear by being in situations where I was forced to talk. I took the initiative in speaking to people and making conversation. In high school, I made a tremendous step in determination and joined the Thespian Club. This was a group that studied drama and members auditioned for performances. I was in several plays but fear was always an overriding factor. Although the audiences were small, I was scared to death! I prayed for God's strength each time and barely survived!

I entered adulthood with the same limitation of fear. Although I became a Christian at the age of nine and taught Sunday school from the time I was fifteen, this fear raged within me. God wanted to show His power but I was content to use His strength as a partial crutch to help me limp along. I prayed for His strength, and then attempted to overcome this handicap in my way.

In my early twenties, I was involved in a missions group at church. All of the women were young and after we became well acquainted, I found it easy to talk with them. However, a woman moved into our town and became the director of the overall mission organization. She was intent on involving the younger ladies in mission activities. Her first name was Prudye and we thought it was a funny name. We would hide every time we saw Prudye approaching, knowing she was going to ask us to do something in ministry.

The young women of the church developed a rallying cry: "Here comes Prudye, you better run!" When we talked about someone who "got on our nerves" we would call them, "A Prudye." We used the name of PRUDYE in vain! One day Prudye caught me unaware and asked if I would lead the program for a day of prayer, which would involve all ladies of the church. I absolutely did not want to do it, yet I felt obligated. I threatened the younger ladies if they did not attend the meeting to help me.

I was a nervous wreck the day of the program. Several people shared interesting stories and presented missionary needs. When I returned to the podium to call on someone to pray, my mind went blank. The more I tried to recall a name, the more fear rose in my mind. I could not recall even the name of my closest friend who sat next to me. Finally, after an embarrassing silence, I blurted out in a very loud voice the only name that came to my mind, "PRAY, PRUDYE, PRAY!" I thought everyone was going to laugh out loud during Prudye's prayer and it was strangely funny to me as well. (I am afraid the missionaries were not blessed that day by our prayers.) However, Prudye prayed; in time, her intense love of missions inspired me to become more involved in ministry.

Every time I tried to overcome my fear by determination, I failed. However, on August 16, 1986, I had a life-changing experience. God spoke to my heart during a mission service. He said five simple words into my spirit, "I want all of you." I mentally replied to God, "You have all of me; I teach a growing Sunday school class; I am involved in missions." I recounted my "spiritual activities" to God. He repeated the five words. I continued to struggle in my spirit, realizing I had never totally surrendered my life to God's Lordship. I would pick and choose the things I knew I could do without getting out of my comfort zone. Finally, I made the decision to surrender my life to *whatever* God wanted me to do.

As I left the auditorium that day, Satan whispered in my mind, "What if God wants you to lead a prison ministry?" The thought of leading a prison ministry scared me but I knew I could not dictate God's calling. I decided if God wanted me to work with prisoners, I would find someone to train me in jail ministry. Because of the total commitment of my life, I no longer had the privilege of choosing my service. As best I could, I was going to do exactly what God led me to do. The one thing I felt certain God would not ask was for me to speak to a large group of people since He knew my limitations and fear.

Exactly three months later, God orchestrated a situation where I had to speak at a denominational gathering of over a thousand people. I cannot begin to tell you how frightened I was. My heart was racing, my mouth as dry as cotton, and my legs felt like spaghetti noodles. As the time grew closer for me to speak, I had a heart-to-heart talk with the Lord. I said, "God, I told you three months ago I would do whatever you asked me to do, but I never dreamed it would be speaking. This is not my idea; if I get up there and faint, I'm going to be really mad." (I realize this was not the most spiritual prayer ever spoken but it was from the heart.)

It was time to go to the podium and I had to ascend four steps. I was desperately afraid my legs would buckle. However, with my first step, God completely removed the raging fear that plagued my life. Before He could take the fear away, I had to give Him my life, all of it. He chose to use me in an area where I had to be totally dependant on Him. He filled me with strength in the weakest place of my life. The ragged fear has never returned and I am grateful to God for His blessing.

> "Now to Him who is able to do exceeding abundantly beyond all that we ask or think, according to the power that works within us, to Him be the glory in the church and in Christ Jesus to all generations forever and ever." (Ephesians 3:20-21)

Little did I know God would place me in a speaking ministry, of all things! God ordained the establishment of Care Ministries. Ann and I have been privileged to speak to thousands of people, sharing the gospel and challenging people to grow spiritually. Obedience to God is a never-ending adventure. He has the right to choose the service, I have the responsibility to participate in His power, and then His peace takes the place of fear. **"The work of righteousness will be peace."** (Isaiah 32:17)

Step 5: Peace

Once you have surrendered the problem in prayer and completed the task required of you, God desires to give you peace. If you worry after surrender, you have not truly surrendered the situation to Him. God wants to give us rest in the knowledge He is working, even when His work is not obvious.

Mary rested in the ability of Jesus to remedy the situation at the wedding feast. The result was overflowing wine! God's resources are always more than we need. He is our Heavenly Father, we are His children and He wants us to trust Him.

- Does the child of good parents worry about whether he will have food each day?
- Does he badger his parents, afraid they are not able to take care of him?
- What fears and worries keep you from experiencing peace?
- Do you think God is able to handle your problem?
- Will you trust God to do what is best in your situation?

A little girl in Middle Tennessee became terribly afraid there were bears in her room. (There are no bears in Middle Tennessee.) She would cry and scream at bedtime, dreading the thought of having bears in her room. At first, the parents talked with her and allowed her to sleep in their room, thinking the fear would go away. This situation continued for some time.

The father finally decided it was time for her to confront the fear of imaginary bears and insisted she sleep in her own room. The parents assured her there were no bears. However, she cried herself to sleep for three nights.

On the fourth night, the father could take the crying no longer. He unlocked his gun safe, removed his shotgun, checked to make sure it was unloaded and went to the daughter's room. He asked his sobbing daughter to tell him when she saw a bear. She pointed to an imaginary bear and the father pointed the gun in that direction and yelled, "BOOM." He asked if there were any others and pretended to shoot all the bears. Finally, she did not see any more. He said, "Well, daddy is going to get all the bears, BOOM, BOOM, BOOM. You do not have to worry about bears any more." The little girl never mentioned bears again. Why? It is because she trusted her daddy to take care of her fears.

We can trust our Heavenly Father to guide us through the barrier of fear and worry. He longs for His children to trust His love, accept His ways, and live in peace. Such a life is a testimony of God's power and is truly beyond the ordinary!

"Be anxious for nothing, but in everything by prayer and supplication with thanksgiving let your requests be made known to God. And the peace of God, which surpasses all comprehension, will guard your hearts and minds in Christ Jesus." (Philippians 4:6-7)

Chapter 3

Greed's Grasp

"For where your treasure is, there your heart will be also."
Matthew 6:21

Section 1

Following the Call

I awoke recently to the national news story of a riot in California during the early morning hours. It was not racial nor was it due to profiling. Shoppers lined up for several days in the parking lot of a mall awaiting their chance to buy the upgraded version of an electronic game debuting before Christmas. As the opening hour approached at the store, people began jockeying for position near the door. The limited number of available games led the crowd to begin pushing and shoving. Police were called and as they lined people against a wall, the riot erupted. Several people were injured and some were arrested. Later in the day, news began to filter out of Connecticut that several shoppers in line there had been robbed of the cash they were planning to use to buy the game.

As the five hundred dollar upgrade became available, the Internet began to hum with bids on the limited number. One game reportedly sold for $9,000! We might dismiss this story as simply one of supply and demand, but there is something deeply disturbing about the behavior. What motivates people to camp for days in a store parking lot? Why engage in a fistfight over an electronic game?

Contrast this with another story I heard the same day. Carolyn and I were helping pack shoeboxes for Operation Christmas Child (sponsored by Samaritan's Purse). The lady coordinating the project for our church shared that she received extensive training for her job. The trainees were told in many countries when a child receives his box, he takes one gift from it and tries to return the box. The recipients must be encouraged to keep their boxes because they are excited with just one gift. I was saddened by the contrast of our culture with so much of the world.

Greed is another barrier to the extraordinary life of faith and adventure God desires for His people. A visit to Webster's New World Dictionary reveals a more extensive definition of greed than a simple thirst for money. "Greed is a desire for more than a person needs or deserves." Greed can affect many areas of life in addition to wealth and possessions. We can be greedy with our time, privacy, family, or spiritual salvation. Looking at limited resources, our greed to retain what we have prevents God from multiplying the supply and using us. *Affluence can become a stumbling block to the abundance God desires for us.*

"The thief comes only to steal and kill and destroy; I came that they may have life, and have it abundantly." (John 10:10)

Spiritual abundance rather than simple affluence is God's desire, and real abundance is much more than material and visible. Abundance in Christ includes the joy of salvation, the peace of reconciliation, and usefulness in ministry. Jesus walked among us to identify with us but also to provide a model for the fullness of life God desires for His children.

A high school senior applied for college and began completing her application. She had to answer several questions, but one deeply disturbed her. The question simply asked, "Are you a leader?" Sadly but truthfully the girl responded, "No," on the application and prepared for rejection. A few weeks later she received a letter from the college. "Congratulations, you have been accepted as a student at our institution. We received applications from 856 leaders. We are thrilled to have one follower." To overcome greed, God simply asks that we be *followers* of the great leader He provided in His Son Jesus. In this chapter we will look at the life of unselfish ministry Jesus exemplified in Mark 5:21-34, the story of Jairus' daughter and the woman with the issue of blood.

Objections to Ministry

Selfishly, Christians find ways to excuse themselves from the service of ministry. We are secure in our salvation, confident of our theology, and comfortable in our righteousness. If we are regular in church attendance and giving, we assume God requires nothing more. Consequently, the bulk of our time and energy is spent pursuing career, family, hobbies, and friendships. While there is nothing inherently wrong with any of these pursuits, this is not the lifestyle of radical obedience that overcomes the ordinary life; it is living in the grasp of greed.

Inconvenient

The first objection to ministry is that it is inconvenient. Human need seldom surfaces at an easily scheduled time. Jesus was a busy man during his three years of ministry. At times, he was sleep deprived, homeless, and unsure of where the next meal would be served or what it would be. As our story begins, Jesus was emerging from the country of the Garasenes where he had ministered to the demon-possessed man. His ministry there had met with such opposition, he was asked to leave. He had quieted the storm on the sea the night before his arrival at Garasenes, so he had been without restful sleep or peaceful surroundings for a long period of time.

"When Jesus had crossed over again in the boat to the other side, a large crowd gathered around Him; and so He stayed by the seashore." (Mark 5:21)

He traveled to the other side of the lake, in all likelihood, hoping to find a good meal and quiet rest. Immediately, a crowd surrounds Him but Jesus did not try to avoid the attention or the needs of the people. The Gospel of Mark refers to the group that met Jesus as a "large crowd." I think of a large crowd as perhaps a church auditorium or fellowship hall filled with people. This group may have been more like a sports arena or stadium full of people. Can you imagine how much human need was represented in this multitude? When Jesus saw the group, he chose to stay precisely because there was great need.

In 1998, Carolyn and I were privileged to lead a spiritual growth retreat for a group of missionary wives in Costa Rica. I remember one missionary woman who lamented their personnel had automobiles to drive. She said, "We could meet so many more people if we rode the city buses. When you're in a car, you are insulated from the crowd." She had the pure heart of a missionary, the heart of ministry exhibited by Christ during His years on earth. Conversely, we often avert our eyes from beggars or cross the street to prevent being asked for a favor. Striving to insulate ourselves from misery, we change schools, neighborhoods and even cities.

NBC television recently did a special on *Rude America*. They placed an eight-month pregnant woman on a subway to observe her treatment by the other passengers. Time after time, no one gave her a place to sit. Occasionally, a man would jump up and offer his seat, but most of the time people not only kept their seats, they refused to look at her. She stood during the subway ride, holding onto a strap while healthy people remained seated.

When he was in college, my son worked as a runner for a law office in downtown Chattanooga. He was an eighteen-year-old, small town boy but because he was required to wear a dress shirt and tie, he appeared to be a professional. A few days into his job, Rad called me with a question. "Mom, what do I do about all the people on the streets asking me for money? Every time I make a run to the courthouse, I'm approached by people needing bus fare or wanting money for food." Not wanting to discourage his willing and giving spirit, I knew some of those folks were scamming him, and he was living on limited income. I advised him to leave his billfold at the office and simply place the money he wanted to give away that day in his pocket. Once he had given away his cash, Rad could truthfully say he had no money. The answer seemed to satisfy him. God does not expect us to give away everything we have or try to meet all the needs we encounter. He does, however, expect us to inconvenience ourselves for others and to meet the needs He impresses into our heart daily. In other words, He does expect us to be willing to give away something!

Americans are more cautious with time than they are with money, comfort and privacy. In a quest for balance in life, time management has become of paramount importance. Americans hate interruptions because "to do" lists govern our decisions. When confronted with an opportunity to minister, many would reply, "I barely have time to complete the things in my life that *must* be done. Don't mention ministry or missions to me; maybe later on in life when the children are grown and I'm retired." Sounds logical but the problem is that it's not Biblical. *A radically different life requires radically different values and behavior.*

"If a brother or sister is without clothing and in need of daily food, and one of you says to them, 'Go in peace, and be warmed and be filled,' and yet you do not give them what is necessary for their body, what use is that? Even so faith, if it has no works, is dead being by itself." (James 2:15-17)

When my husband and I were young parents, we experienced the time crunch of Sunday morning preparations for church. Our children were three years apart, so we had a baby and a toddler to wake, feed, bathe, and dress. There was always the mishap at the last minute like a dirty diaper or spilled milk. Usually we were exhausted and pushed to the limit as we packed everyone into the car for the drive to church. One Sunday we were especially pressed for time; as we pulled out of the garage, heavy rain flooded the street. At the first stoplight, a car was stalled, blocking the intersection. The driver was outside, hood open, tinkering with the engine. He was rain drenched with no hat or coat and clearly frustrated. With no approaching traffic, we could have easily pulled around him and proceeded to church. My husband asked, "Do you think we should stop?" "Sure," I responded. "But, we'll be late for church," he lamented. Quickly, without thinking, I said, "What use is church if you can't stop and help somebody on the way?" We stopped, picked up the man and he immediately water soaked our seat and floorboard. We took him to his church to call for help. We were late for church that day, but I had more joy in attending than I had experienced in a long time.

Again, God does not ask us to meet every need we encounter, but He does expect us to care for the one needy person He appoints. Returning to the story in Mark, one man named Jairus, in the midst of the multitude, is able to capture Jesus' attention.

> **"One of the synagogue officials named Jairus came up, and on seeing Him, fell at His feet and implored Him earnestly, saying, 'My little daughter is at the point of death; please come and lay Your hands on her, so that she will get well and live.' And He went off with him..."** (Mark 5:22-24a)

Jesus' ministry to the large group is interrupted by Jairus, but He is compelled to go with him to see his daughter. On His way, Jesus is again interrupted by another need, a woman with an issue of blood. Here was an interruption wrapped inside another interruption. Sounds like most Mondays!

> **"...and a large crowd was following Him and pressing in on Him. A woman who had had a hemorrhage for twelve years, and had endured much at the hands of many physicians, and had spent all that she had and was not helped at all, but rather had grown worse—after hearing about Jesus, she came up in the crowd behind Him and touched His cloak. For she thought, 'If I just touch His garments, I will get well.'"** (Mark 5:24b-28)

In like manner, God sometimes confronts us with more than one need. It may be a multifaceted, prolonged situation. Several years ago, I had a tenant named Rick (name has been changed). I knew when Rick moved into my apartments he had been in several questionable situations personally and legally, but his Christian parents urged me to give him a chance. Rick was a recovering alcoholic, took numerous medications, and drew government disability, which gave him extra time to get into mischief. He rented for about two years with no serious problems. Inevitably, he fell off the wagon and caused quite a stir with his neighbors when he asked a married woman for a date. I called his father, and he moved Rick to another apartment complex.

I had been kind and longsuffering during Rick's two years of tenancy and thought my responsibility to him had ended. However, when he left, I told Rick if I could help him overcome his alcohol problem to call me. Several months later, he called and asked if I would transport him to Nashville, ninety miles away, to alcohol detox. I told him I would when he was accepted. This decision was not popular with my children, who responded by saying, "You won't drive him by yourself!" Well, I took care of that problem by asking Carolyn to go with me.

A few days later Rick called my cell phone when I was forty-five miles away from home saying he needed me to transport him immediately. Carolyn and I dropped everything, drove for an hour, and found Rick quite inebriated. He was a sight, red-eyes, baseball cap over his kinky hair, cigarette hanging out of his mouth, standing at the side of the road holding a garbage bag full of clothes and toiletries. At this point, Carolyn and I learned a patient will not be accepted into alcohol detox unless he is drunk. Rick had certainly done his part to insure admission! Although it was bitterly cold, we had to keep the car windows partially rolled down during the trip. The smell of alcohol in the car was so strong we were afraid of becoming inebriated ourselves!

Rick was in a relaxed state and began to talk. He shared with us about previous relationships, his daughter, and his mental problems. I learned for the first time Rick was bipolar and schizophrenic, the reason for much of his medication. He began to brag about some of his exploits and then said, "Yea, some people say they're crazy, but I've got the papers to prove it." After that statement, Carolyn and I kept a close eye on the rear view mirror, watching Rick's every move. Our only comfort was the knowledge God had appointed us for this mission.

Finally, arriving at the detox facility, we learned Rick had to be evaluated before he could be admitted. I nearly panicked thinking we might have to transport him back home in the same state. The nurse told us to go eat dinner and return two hours later for the verdict. Much to our relief, he was accepted, but he needed cash for snacks and phone calls. Rick had no money, so I gave him what I had before we left. I probably would have paid any amount to insure we left him. I learned that night in a new way how ministry can be inconvenient, expensive, and nerve wracking. At the same time, I knew we were in the center of God's will during the process. Rick returned home within a month and still struggles with his problems, but success is in God's hands, not ours. *Christ asks that we be authentic in our witness, which often requires doing, not talking.*

Draining

Another objection Christians use to avoid ministry is that it is draining. My daughter had a favorite expression during her high school days, "These people just wear me out." Needy people are draining. They can wear us out! Often in ministry we are drained of spiritual power, time, money, and other resources by the overwhelming nature of the problems we encounter. We must constantly go back to our power source, the Holy Spirit. Jesus had a similar experience in His encounter with the woman in Mark chapter five.

> "For she thought, 'If I just touch His garments, I will get well.' Immediately the flow of her blood was dried up; and she felt in her body that she was healed of her affliction. Immediately Jesus, perceiving in Himself that the power proceeding from Him had gone forth, turned around in the crowd and said, 'Who touched My garments?'" (Mark 5:28-30)

Jesus had a physical manifestation of the spiritual when the woman touched His garment. Carolyn told me several years after my divorce that during my most emotional times of sharing, she actually felt something drain out of her as she ministered to me. From the depths of who we are in Christ, we must be willing to give to a lost and needy world. But let me offer a word of caution. Many in our world, even fellow Christians need personal encouragement, prayer, and time. However, there is a difference between purely emotional neediness and spiritual neediness. There are some individuals who exhibit a dysfunctional, emotional neediness that is a black hole, never to be filled by another person. They, too, can drain us of time, resources, emotional support, and even our selfhood if we allow it. Such individuals usually need professional counseling more than simple companionship.

While we should pray for and encourage all people, God must clearly direct us to those individuals to whom we give in-depth ministry and time. Ministry for the sake of "doing something" can become fruitless if it is not God directed because appearances can sometimes be deceiving.

My brother is a retired Army colonel, a physician, and a professor at a well-known university hospital in the Southeast. He is not wealthy, but definitely has ample income, drawing two salaries. Jim and his wife, Becky, have five children ranging in age from twelve to twenty-three. None are married, so they continue to take a family vacation every summer. This past year they were on an extended road trip in their older fifteen-passenger van. One day, after several hours driving, the family of seven rolled out at a popular fast-food restaurant. They had been vacationing all week, were dressed casually, and most had been sleeping as they drove. They probably resembled a band of gypsies as they climbed out of their vehicle and descended in mass on the restaurant. Due to eating out three meals a day, my brother placed the family on a strict budget for lunch. They were instructed to order from the $1 menu, no more than $3.00 per person.

My brother gave Becky his order and disappeared to the restroom. She was talking to the children and assembling the order for seven, at the same time limiting them to $3.00. Suddenly a man walked up to her and said, "Can I be of service?" She was confused as to what he meant, and then he handed her $40.00. She still was not understanding his intent when he said, "Don't worry about it, it's a God-thing." He then hurriedly left the restaurant. My dumbfounded sister-in-law was left holding the $40.00 when Jim returned from the bathroom. As she told him the story, he chuckled and said, "Well, that's combos for everyone." Then he began to evaluate their appearance and decided they must look pretty pitiful! They, of course, did not spend the money, later giving it away to someone in real need.

We cannot decide by appearances the recipients of our ministry. The Spirit must direct us to the individuals He has prepared us to help. Otherwise, we are wasting valuable resources and will quickly become drained. Conversely, we can be surrounded by real need and become calloused and spiritually blind to it. Our pastor shares the experience of being invited as the revival speaker at a small church in North Carolina. After the Sunday morning worship service, everyone was asked to attend a dinner on the grounds at the church picnic area. Being a family-oriented church, each family group occupied a table or area under the pavilion. The pastor shared the meal was well underway, and he was left standing alone with nothing to eat and nowhere to sit. Finally, someone noticed his exclusion and encouraged him to eat with his family. If a leader can go unnoticed, what about a stranger? In our efforts to avoid being drained by the world, we often fail to look around us and evaluate who might need us.

Inadequate resources

When faced with overwhelming needs and limited resources, Christians are tempted to do nothing. At this point, a radical dependence upon God and His resources is required for effective ministry. We may have limited time, money, and space, but God's resources in Christ are unlimited and eternal. There will always be adequate resources for what He directs us to do. Logically, it made no sense for Jesus to stop for a woman who had been sick for twelve years when a child was dying. Her situation was certainly not an emergency, and Jairus had to wonder *why* Jesus would allow himself to be diverted. However, Jesus knew:

- The Heavenly Father was in control.
- The time was adequate for everything the Father had appointed Him to do.
- His deviation from the path to Jairus' daughter was Spirit directed.
- God was with the little girl when He was not.
- God could raise her from the dead if necessary.

Why do we doubt God's resources for life? Even the faith of a small child can put us to shame. Children do not get up in the morning doubting the ability of the parent to care for their needs. They simply expect their needs to be met. My daughter Michelle invited me to eat dinner with her recently. My granddaughter, Skylar, was busily playing in the kitchen, singing songs and practicing cheerleading. Out of curiosity I asked Skylar what Michelle was preparing for dinner. She said, "I don't know, but it will be something." She continued enjoying her time, confident her hunger would be satisfied. (This is the same child I had earlier asked, "What is your favorite food?" Her reply, "I eat dinner for chocolate!")

A few years ago, a retired minister and his wife visited our church. Carolyn and I struck up a conversation with them after worship service and invited them to our Sunday school class. They began to share with us about their pastorate in a nearby rural church. The pastor's wife told us about a young child in their church approximately four years old. This girl saw a commercial on television encouraging people to give to the hungry children in a third world country, and pictures were shown of the emaciated victims of famine. The youngster became so burdened for the hungry children that every Sunday she would go to the altar, cry and pray for them. Her weeping disturbed the adults in the church, and they decided to join our denomination's efforts to combat world hunger. They promised to match every penny the children in the church raised for this cause. The pastor's wife shared the children were so excited about this ministry that over $30,000 was raised in two years. These children did not examine the resources but rather focused on the need. Why can't we be more like them?

God does not ask us to feed all the children of the world, but He does ask us to minister to those He sends. In Carolyn's family, God sent Luke Harrison Castle to be adopted and loved, and He may send you into a ministry for neglected children. Our former county mayor spoke briefly when our church celebrated its fiftieth anniversary. She shared about a visit to one of our public elementary schools where she spoke. After Nancy Allen finished her speech, a young girl came up and asked if she attended church. Nancy assured the child that she did. The child continued to ask the same question. Finally, Nancy said, "Why do you keep asking me if I attend church?" The little child answered sadly, "I wish I could go to church." How many children are there in your community whose heart's desire is to attend church? God may send you to transport one or to begin a bus ministry in your area. If He does, He will provide the resources needed.

Your personal finances may also be inadequate for family needs. You may feel tithing or giving toward missions and ministry is impossible. Be assured God will bless your family financially when you practice sacrificial giving. In fact, the problem with your finances may stem from self-centered living. When my son graduated from high school, God opened the door for me to leave the town where we had lived twenty-four years.

Our house, which was paid for, sold quickly but the proceeds were split with the children's father. Child support ended and I took on a house payment in the same timeframe with two children in college. My income changed drastically, and at the same time, the apartment business entered a recession. I was frightened. One night, I turned the television to a religious programming channel, and the speaker said the solution to financial reversals was to start giving more. It made no sense from the human standpoint, but I felt God nudge me. I began giving more money away, and God worked through a difficult period in my finances. Every time I was short on making my bills, a conference would be added to our calendar. The honorariums bridged the gap in my finances. Unexpectedly, a woman in our denomination sent $1,000 to our ministry. When I stopped fearing my inadequacy, God sent the resources for every need.

Outcomes from Ministry

Healing

We are not to engage in ministry to make ourselves feel better. *Jesus sends us into the world to touch others with healing so they will be better.*

"And His disciples said to Him, 'You see the crowd pressing in on You, and You say, 'Who touched Me?' And He looked around to see the woman who had done this. But the woman fearing and trembling, aware of what had happened to her, came and fell down before Him and told Him the whole truth. And He said to her, 'Daughter, your faith has made you well; go in peace and be healed of your affliction.'" (Mark 5:31-34)

The woman had a small, even superstitious faith. The size of her faith did not diminish the bigness of God's mercy. It was not so much her touch but whom she touched. *We are not sent to heal the world but to point the world to the Healer.* For a hurting world, we represent the fringe of Jesus' garment. As they touch us, they find healing from Him. Please do not be afraid to touch and be touched as God directs.

Several years ago, I had a young renter named Philip (name changed). He was only nineteen and had a police record. His boss from a neighboring business asked me to give him a chance by renting to him, and I agreed. Philip did fine for a while, went to work, and paid his rent. One weekend he took his employer's truck for a joy ride and blew his rent on alcohol. By Monday morning, he was broke, out of a job and facing possible arrest. He feared I would be asking him to move.

Philip was a child of bitter divorce but never complained. I chatted with his mother once on the phone and she told me neither parent had wanted Philip or his brother. Their father would take them to a neighboring state for visits. Returning them to Tennessee, he would let them out of the car miles from their mother's house. He knew if they were returned to the mother directly, she would refuse to take them.

I helped Philip through his legal problems, and he was able to stay in his apartment for a few more weeks. Finally, with no work he was forced to move. The last time I saw Philip, he gave me the apartment key, and we walked down the steps together. Suddenly I heard God say to me, "Tell him you wish he had been your little boy." I felt a surge of tenderness toward this young man and I said, "Philip, I wish you had been my little boy. Things would have been different." He looked at me and said, "I wish you had been my mother. May I hug you?" We warmly embraced. For that moment, in that touch, I knew God was reaching out to Philip with healing.

Do not be afraid to touch someone when God leads. You will be the healing they need for that moment. I have a dear friend whose baby is dying. He was oxygen deprived for nine minutes at birth and is brain dead. God in His mercy has sent a dear older woman to this home. She comes five days a week, arriving at nine in the morning and stays until late afternoon. She holds the baby all day when the mother is caring for her other child, her husband and her home. God asks us to touch and hold a dying world to learn and share compassion. I would rather be the one willing to touch and hold than distancing myself because of fear. What about you?

Relationship

Jesus called the woman with the issue of blood out of the crowd and questioned her. He did this, not to embarrass the woman, but to form a relationship with her. Notice in verse 34 He called her "daughter." He desires for us to minister out of a relationship with a person. *Ministry is about people not projects.* We are to be more than a food pantry and a clothes closet. Jesus says He is our friend, and He wants us to befriend those who need Him to bring them to a faith relationship.

Ron Phillips once said, "God wants to give us a relationship, not an assignment." Not only is ministry to result in relationship, ministry IS our relationship with Jesus Christ. We are His eyes, His hands, and His feet. God desires that we ask Him to see the world as He sees it. Once we do, we will view people not as *bad* but as *lost*. Once we perceive people's neediness rather than their faults, it becomes easier to involve ourselves in their lives with love and forgiveness.

Civic clubs and community organizations are involved in wonderful programs to help people. But only Spirit-led ministry can draw a lost person into a relationship with Jesus Christ. When I was a young mother, a national club for women was formed in our community. They had wonderful community service projects, and many of my friends joined. My best friend at the time urged me to become a member. One day I responded, "If I am going to do service, I would rather do it through my church than a civic organization." She responded, "Well, you don't do it there either." I quickly answered, "Well, I guess I just don't want to do it at all." If service to others is *work*, we will lose interest. However, if we allow God to use ministry to form relationships, it will be exciting, fruitful, and rewarding. I am grateful God moved me beyond seeing ministry as a work project. *Ministry is a relationship in progress.*

Ministry that flows from a spiritual fountain is alive and real. God has given me many opportunities to minister to my renters because of our special relationship. I try to cultivate a friendship with each tenant. By meeting needs when I can, tenants allow me to enter their lives in meaningful ways. At Christmas I give each person a coupon for ten dollars off January rent and enclose a Gospel tract with the card. My mother once jokingly said, "You bribe them to read the tract." That is okay if they read it! The birth of a child, a wedding, graduation, or death of a loved one is an entry point into another's life to show God's love. Take advantage of happy, as well as sad times, to minister to those around you. As God nudges, respond to His leading.

I have also been the recipient of God prompting others to minister to me. I recently experienced a severe stomach virus. Living alone, I did not realize how truly sick I was. Every sip of liquid I swallowed was eventually lost, and I developed a fever. Carolyn and I were expecting house guests from East Tennessee to stay in our homes for the weekend. When I became ill, she had to entertain the entire group at her house; she was unable to monitor my condition. I rapidly became disoriented and dizzy. I would try to get out of bed and move to the couch, but after a few minutes I could no longer sit upright. I would then drag myself back to bed. The afternoon of my second day of illness, a friend of mine who is nurse, called to chat. She had not telephoned for months and immediately realized I was sick. When I explained my dizziness, she concluded I was dehydrated. I immediately called my daughter, who is also a nurse. She came to my house, set up IV fluids, and spent the night. I later asked my friend, Vickie, why she had called that particular day. She said God had prompted her to check on me. A persistent thought about someone is probably a nudge from God for a reason. Be sensitive to His voice because He wants to heal, bless and rescue needy people around you through relationships.

Witness

A third outcome from ministry should be an opportunity to witness of our faith in Jesus Christ. Often God uses our weaknesses and sorrows as a platform to witness of His power to sustain and heal. I never share about my divorce during a conference that someone does not respond. Many have thanked me for being willing to share and become vulnerable. Almost every family has been touched by divorce in our society.

What problem has God allowed into your life? It may be God's avenue to use you to help another person. Nothing enters a Christian's life outside the providential care of God. Your sorrow is in His will for discipline and service. Be willing to share your story, the lessons learned, and the means of coping.

"For just as the sufferings of Christ are ours in abundance, so also our comfort is abundant through Christ. But if we are afflicted, it is for your comfort and salvation, or if we are comforted, it is for your comfort, which is effective in the patient enduring of the same sufferings which we also suffer; and our hope for you is firmly grounded, knowing that as you are sharers of our sufferings, so also you are sharers of our comfort." (II Corinthians 1:5-7)

A couple in our church lost their nineteen-year-old son in a tragic automobile accident. He was a good student, hard worker, and fine Christian young man. They have grieved, but they have also reached out to other families experiencing the loss of a child. They are using tragedy as a means to witness of God's power to sustain. I have often said the loss of a child seems the hardest pain that can be inflicted upon a parent. If I had to go through it, I would want this couple at my side.

As Christians, we are hesitant to share a verbal testimony and lead another individual to Christ. It should not be so difficult. All God asks of us is to testify of His power to change a life, our life. *Witnessing is sharing your story. Ministry is sharing your life: giving of who you are and what you have.* It is so simple a child can do it. Often, children do it best.

My grandmother died in 2004, at age ninety-eight. It was intriguing to sit and listen to her stories of childhood, marriage, and the many struggles of a long life. She did not meet her mother until she arrived in heaven because her biological mother died a few days after giving birth. Gran (as we lovingly called her) also lost three brothers in infancy or early childhood. During those days of primitive medicine many children died. An epidemic of diphtheria swept the community, and Gran's best friend, Eloise, became ill. The girls were not old enough to attend school and were accustomed to playing together daily. Gran's stepmother warned her to stay away from her friend's house since the disease was contagious. Grandmother loved Eloise so much she could not bear separation and would slip out, climb through the window of the other home, crawl into her friend's bed and sleep with her. Several days later the little girl died.

Grandmother was too young to understand the full meaning of all that had happened. Her stepmother broke the news to Gran and told her that her friend's family had no dress in which to bury her. Gran immediately went to her closet, took out her best Sunday dress, and gave it to the family for the burial. Gran was not old enough to attend school, yet she knew all about ministry.

- She loved without regard for safety.
- She risked disapproval.
- She gave the best she had.

I want to be more like my grandmother. I want to be more like the model Jesus gave us in the fifth chapter of Mark.

"And entering in, He said to them, "Why make a commotion and weep? The child has not died, but is asleep." (Mark 5:39)

This is the good news of the Gospel; people do not have to experience eternal death. This is what Christ asks us to share through our witness and ministry. For adults, busyness and distraction become the enemies of ministry.

My mother passed away in 2001, from cancer. She battled valiantly for nine years with my father faithfully by her side. She had been the homemaker during their fifty-three years of married life, but the last two years I saw her turn the household duties over to him, one by one. He not only nursed her better than any professional could have done, he cleaned, cooked, and maintained a spotless home.

During her last hours my sister and I were on the road trying to get to her bedside, but my brother was there to relate her passing. He said Daddy was taking care of everyone present by serving breakfast and cleaning the kitchen. My brother, a pulmonary specialist, realized my mother was entering her last few minutes. Her breaths were coming ever more slowly and were shallow. He hurried to the kitchen to get my father. "If you want to see your wife again alive, come now." My father rushed to the bedroom, and he and Jim held her hands until she stopped breathing. His busyness in the kitchen almost deprived my father of his wife's last moments. So is all of life on this earth. The Great Physician is calling us to proceed to the bedside of a lost and dying world.

Section 2

Seeing the Ministry

Ann and I were excited about the invitation to lead our first weekend retreat. At the same time, we were somewhat intimidated by the group. This was a large association of churches and we desperately wanted the weekend to go well. However, in preparation for the retreat, we spent more time planning our wardrobe than we did preparing our hearts. We wanted to make a good impression and were overly concerned about what to wear.

The night before the retreat, I packed a suitcase and hang-up bag since we were leaving early the next morning. I also checked the media equipment and was assured everything was ready for the trip. I went to bed after setting my alarm clock for 3:00 a.m.

The alarm sounded and I jumped out of bed. I decided to wear jeans and old tennis shoes to be comfortable driving. I awoke my husband at 4:00, telling him I was ready to leave. He stumbled out of bed and mumbled he would help load the car. He told me to get the media equipment and he would put the clothes in the trunk.

Ann and I traveled several hours and were approaching the remote retreat camp when a sickening thought crossed my mind. I could not remember seeing my suitcase in the trunk. I asked Ann if she noticed it but she had not. She attempted to calm my mind, and I tried to convince myself Danny loaded my clothes in the car as he had promised. Not being able to shake the nagging thought, I stopped the car and opened the trunk. No suitcase! My hang-up bag was there but not my luggage.

I began to panic and told Ann my dilemma. Time would not allow me to return to the nearest town to purchase replacement items. Ann asked, "What are you missing?" Almost hysterical, I replied, "EVERYTHING!" "What specific things?" Ann asked. I began to recount the things in my suitcase. I mentioned makeup-she said I could use hers and on and on she offered; hair dryer-I could use hers, hair brushes-I could use hers, knee-highs-she had extras, underwear-she had six pairs. After a few minutes, she calmed my fears by supplying all I needed to wear for the weekend. At this point, I was quite amazed Ann had packed two of everything.

Suddenly, I noticed my worn out tennis shoes and panic struck again. "What am I going to wear for shoes?" I asked. Ann quietly replied with a question, "What color shoes had you planned to wear?" "Taupe," I said. Concern flooded my mind. I had a mental picture of leading the conference barefooted. Much to my surprise Ann said, "I have two pairs of taupe shoes." "Why in the world would you bring two pairs of taupe shoes?" I questioned. "For such a time as this," was her quick answer.

Ann is a very organized person but this goes over the edge, two pairs of shoes exactly alike! Yet, I was grateful she brought an extra pair. She asked what size I wore and we concluded my size 5 ½ feet would have to manage in her size 7 shoes. We arrived at the retreat center thinking my problem had been solved.

After finding our room, we began to dress for the retreat. All went well until I tried on the shoes. My feet were sliding around in them and I felt like I was on skis. Like a blast from the past, I remembered how I put Kleenex in my children's shoes until they could "grow into them." God had gone before us because there was a box of tissues in our room. I began to stuff Ann's shoes until the box was empty. (I guess the housekeeper thought we had a terrible cold to use an entire box of tissues.) I told Ann, "If the women get emotional tonight, I can take off my shoes and pass them around the room; there would be plenty of tissues for everyone."

While walking to the meeting hall, I had a terrible time keeping my "skis" straight. We finally reached the room where the women were waiting and I made Ann enter first. I closely followed, locking my knees and sliding my feet along to prevent the shoes from falling off. They were making scraping noises across the floor but there was nothing I could do about the sound. I only hoped everyone knew the sound was coming from the shoes! After all my concern about trying to impress the ladies, I was walking like a zombie and worried about losing a shoe. After seeing the questioning looks on the ladies faces, I told them the story. After the laughter died down, we proceeded with the retreat. The story actually "broke the ice" and broke my pride at the same time!

I had been more concerned about my appearance than I was about God's purpose for the weekend. Ann and I learned a lesson that weekend; the most important thing is serving God and not impressing people. I majored on a minor setback and overlooked the main reason for my being at the retreat. How often do we overlook our reason for living and slip into a life of selfishness? How often do we overlook people because our eyes are on ourselves? If we are to overcome the barrier of greed and self, we must begin to see people as Jesus sees them. For this to take place, we must first catch a vision of Jesus working in our lives.

We often sing about wanting to see Jesus. We want to experience Him in uplifting, warm and fuzzy ways. We want our *lives* touched but our *lifestyles* left unchanged. However, Jesus told us how we see him most clearly:

"For I was hungry, and you gave me something to eat; I was thirsty, and you gave Me drink; I was a stranger, and you invited me in; naked, and you clothed Me; I was sick, and you visited me; I was in prison, and you came to Me.' Then the righteous will answer Him, saying, 'Lord, when did we see You hungry, and feed you, thirsty, and give You drink? And when did we see You a stranger, and invite You in, or naked, and clothe You? And when did we see You sick, or in prison, and come to You?' And the King will answer and say to them, 'Truly I say to you, to the extent that you did it to one of these brothers of Mine, even the least of them, you did it to Me.'" (Matthew 25:35-40)

We are to worship the Living God for He is worthy to be praised. He deserves and desires to be worshipped. However, that is only the beginning. *Our worship finds its worth as we work out our faith in obedience to His voice.* Do you have people in your realm of influence who are the "least of these"? They are the multitudes of people we often refuse to see.

- The smelly homeless
- The rebellious teenager
- The struggling waitress
- The lonely neighbor
- The extremely poor
- The unwanted child
- The chronically ill
- The confused immigrant
- The hopelessly lost

Will we continue to sit in our isolated churches and refuse to experience the blessing of ministering in the name of the Lord? Will we miss the opportunity to minister to Jesus in the form of the "least of these" because it gets us too far from our comfort zone? People surround us who need a touch from Jesus but often our selfishness prevents us from seeing them.

Surrounded by Hurts

The suffering of others presents itself almost daily and can be distressing. We are not responsible to minister to the masses. Jesus was surrounded by a multitude of people in Mark 5, yet His gaze fell on two people in need and he ministered to them. He did not heal everyone but He was obedient to the Father's will.

In this account, Jesus raised a twelve-year-old girl (Luke 8:42) from the dead and healed the woman with a twelve-year issue of blood. This is an example of the broad spectrum of ministry that awaits each of us.

- Young and old
- Rich and Poor
- Sudden need and chronic problems
- Religious and the unclean
- The loved and the outcast

Jesus was not distracted by the multitudes following him out of curiosity or even praise. He taught us by example to be keenly aware of people's needs as we travel, work and play daily.

Overwhelming Problems
Television is flooded with news, most of which is filled with human need. The local newspaper informs us about problems of our community. We are personally acquainted with family, friends and neighbors who are besieged with overwhelming situations. Our church family is often suffering emotional hurts that are not shared openly. Almost everyone crossing our path has a problem that weighs upon the heart.

Realizing the significant time and resources required to minister to the needy individual, we have a choice to make. Our human reaction is to look the other way; knowing we cannot do everything, we do nothing. In reality, we do nothing because of our selfishness. We excuse ourselves from ministry because of the magnitude of the problems; yet God is not moved by our excuses.

Years ago, I was squeezing in a grocery stop before picking up my children from school. Entering the store, I saw masses of people, no shopping carts and many frowns. I learned the checkout scanners were not working and cashiers were at a standstill. I should have left but thought they would soon be repaired. I proceeded to hurry through the aisles snatching and grabbing needed items. Almost running down the first aisle, I noticed an attractive, blonde, young woman pushing her cart, shoulders drooping and crying.

God clearly nudged my spirit but I dismissed the prompting due to the lack of time. I saw the woman several times throughout the store and she continued to cry. Each time, God spoke to me about my responsibility to talk with her. My excuses began to flourish.

- I needed to get to the school.
- There were too many people in the store.
- It would embarrass her if I initiated a conversation.
- I might offend her.
- On and on I went with my excuses.

When it was time to check out, the lanes were lined with people halfway to the back of the store. Guess who was standing beside me? God again gave me the opportunity to speak with her. I began to bargain with God. I silently said to the Lord, "Since there is a crowd around us, I don't think I should say anything to her. But if I am here in ten minutes, I will talk with her." Ten minutes passed and we had not moved. I was forced to make another bargain. If I am here another five minutes, it will be my sign. I am ashamed to admit I walked out of the store and never said a word.

Conviction began to eat at my heart because I had been disobedient to a direct command of God. Although I asked forgiveness, the picture of the young woman remained in my mind for months. I prayed for her often but knew I had failed her, failed in my convictions, and most importantly, failed the Lord.

Approximately ten years later, I was leading a conference in a local church on personal ministry. Relating this story, I made a point that it was best to follow God's leadership even when it did not seem appropriate. After the conference, a lady approached the podium and said, "I was the woman in the grocery." I looked at her closely and could see no resemblance to the picture emblazoned on my mind. She had long, dark hair and looked nothing like the blonde, shorthaired woman I carried with me mentally. I even said, "I don't think so." She began to laugh and said, "Oh, back then my hair was blonde and it was very short. I suppose I have changed a lot over the years." Seeing her with those features, I realized it was the same person.

I apologized for failing to follow God's direction that day long ago at the grocery. She began to share the events of that period in her life and they were traumatic. She was married to an abusive man, had three children and the only time she could escape the house was to go grocery shopping. She would go there and cry because she did not want the children to see her upset. She asked if I had time to talk with her privately. I all but dragged her to a Sunday school room, grateful for the opportunity to right a wrong. Unfortunately, we rarely get a second opportunity to minister to the unknown person we meet among the masses. Therefore, we must learn to be obedient, regardless of the overwhelming problems surrounding us.

Our Part

What does God expect of us since we have limited time and resources? He is surely aware we cannot make a dent in the needs of society around us. He knows completely the magnitude of the problems but the Holy Spirit moves us to see the individual. As we follow the Lord's voice, He will open our eyes to the specific person we are called to serve.

We probably have a preference for working in a particular area of need. We may feel comfortable taking food to a homeless shelter but refuse to witness to an elite member of our society. Yet, God desires to grow us spiritually by placing us outside our preference of ministry. *As servants of the Lord, it is not ours to determine the ministry; it is the Holy Spirit who directs us to minister.* God directs by orchestrating divine opportunities for His children to meet the needs of others in His name.

Dr. David Jeremiah shared the following story about a missionary named Barnabas Shaw. Cape Town, South Africa, was a bustling outpost when Barnabas arrived in 1815, intending to preach the Gospel and plant a church. Unfortunately, the authorities controlling the city were hostile to missionary efforts, and Barnabas was banned from engaging in evangelistic work. Not knowing what else to do, he bought a yoke of oxen and a cart, packed his belongings, and headed into the interior, letting the oxen lead the way. On the twenty-seventh day of the trip, he camped for the night near a party of Hottentots who were also traveling through the region. The Hottentots explained they were traveling to Cape Town, hoping to find a missionary to teach the "Great Word."

Had either group started a half-day earlier or later, they would not have met. Had either traveled at a different speed, they would have missed one another. God ordained the encounter and His providence led Barnabas Shaw to his appointed field.

God has uniquely placed us in positions so we can be His witness and minister to a hurting person. Someone is "camping" near us, needing the touch of the Lord Jesus. We are His servants and must be sensitive to divine appointments. God will orchestrate events but we have to be obedient. However, encounters of ministry often cost us something.

- Will we cling to what is ours?
- Are we willing to confess our greed?
- Will we sacrifice to give whatever God asks?
- Are we ready to break the grasp of greed?

Ann and I were traveling to a conference and stopped for lunch. Our waitress greeted us with a smile and was pleasant while taking our order. Soon she disappeared and eventually someone else delivered our food. She never returned and we were somewhat grumpy about the service.

As we were leaving, our waitress was talking on a pay phone and was visibly upset. God whispered in my ear, "She is hurting, minister in My name." She ended her phone conversation and began to sob. I asked if we could help but she continued to cry. She eventually said, "A few minutes ago I received a phone call about my mother. She suffered a massive stroke, and she is not expected to live." We learned her mother lived over three hundred miles away.

God again whispered, "Give her $100.00 so she can make the trip to visit her mother." I selfishly clutched my purse to my side. All it contained was a small sum of money stuffed away for my fast-approaching mission trip to Costa Rica. I silently argued, "But Lord, what about MY trip? I do not have long to raise money for MY trip." God gently nudged my spirit and I knew I had to be obedient.

I asked the waitress if she had the money necessary to visit her mother. (I was secretly hoping to hear, "Yes, I am fine." Maybe God only wanted my willingness.) However, she said, "No, I do not." I gave her $100.00 and she refused to take it, saying she did not even know me. I assured her it was God providing for the trip. Ann and I had prayer with her and I left with three dollars remaining in my mission fund. Yes, ministry will cost something but there is more to the story.

Ann gave me $50.00 saying she wanted to pay half the trip cost of the waitress. Later in the week, God led four people to financially support my mission trip. When I left for Costa Rica, I had sufficient funds-God multiplied the money I gave.

What if I followed my human instincts and clung to my money? I probably would have raked, scraped and found the money to go on the mission trip, but I would have missed seeing God provide. God had a much better plan than mine. He provided for the waitress to visit her dying mother; at the same time, He provided for my trip through others. It was a lesson about how greed challenges generosity. When generosity wins the challenge, God is honored and blessings abound.

Why are we slow to act when the all-knowing God prompts us? Theodore Williams of India said, "We face a humanity that is too precious to neglect." Yet, we do it all the time. It is time for the church to be Christ in the world. It is imperative Christians be known for our love instead of our hate. Only when love validates the witness will Christ become real to the world.

"We know love by this, that He laid down His life for us; and we ought to lay down our lives for the brethren. But whoever has the world's goods, and beholds his brother in need and closes his heart against him, how does the love of God abide in him? Little children, let us not love with word or tongue, but in deed and truth."
(I John 3:16-18)

Hurts Seem Incurable

Looking at society, we are prone to take the pessimistic outlook and conclude, "Things have gone too far." In many situations, Christians have become discouraged and ineffective in influencing the world in which we live.

- Drugs are rampant.
- Children are disobedient.
- Music is suggestive.
- Movies are obscene.
- Political corruption is prevalent.
- Poverty is increasing.
- Sexual immorality is accepted.

How can we possibly address the needs that appear incurable? It is obvious our society is in a downward spiral as we consider the apathy of people toward other human beings. It is shocking to hear a dramatic story of a woman being beaten on the street and neighbors walking past her with no concern. Less dramatic events take place daily and have almost become a normal part of life. Muggings, robbery, rapes, abortions and even school shootings no longer have the shock value they once did. A solution seems hopeless because the problems are so deeply embedded into society.

A few years ago, the teenage pregnancy rate was tremendously high in the county where I live. A professor at the local university became concerned about the number of children having children. She visited several twelve-year-old girls who had recently given birth to babies. Her heart was broken by this and as a Christian, felt God's calling to do something about the problem of teenage sexual promiscuity.

She formed a team to develop an abstinence-based curriculum that would be taught in the middle schools. (This was before the national government began to advocate abstinence programs.) I was asked to serve on the team and readily accepted the challenge. We met and formulated a plan, the first being a survey of high school students concerning their sexual activity.

After completing the survey, we compiled the information and the results were both staggering and upsetting. The survey revealed 78% of high school boys and 64 % of the girls were engaged in premarital sex, with most having multiple partners. I remember walking to my car that night and was suddenly overcome with a cloud of discouragement. I thought, "There is absolutely no way we can change this problem. It is like a huge wave and nothing can stop the tide. Teenage pregnancy will only increase, meaning abortions will increase as well." My hope had been dashed by the statistics and felt the problem was incurable. The curriculum was developed, but I had little faith it would be successful.

Humanly Impossible

"With men this is impossible." (Matthew 19:26b)

Are we to throw up our hands in defeat when the circumstances around us seem incurable? Let's return to our story in Mark 5 where we find the extremes in human hopelessness. One young girl was sick and no one could prevent her death. Another woman suffered from a debilitating illness and the condition only grew worse. She spent all she had on physicians (Sounds like today's medical costs.) These are two examples of the inability of man to cure the problems of another.

The *woman* in the story was discouraged beyond measure. What about you? Your problems may be equal to these situations or at least seem overwhelming. You may personally suffer physically from a condition that seems to have no remedy. You may be emotionally hurt because of a broken relationship. You may be spiritually out of touch with the Lord.

The *family* of the dying girl also suffered a grievous pain. What about your family? Are any sick, emotionally upset or spiritually undone? If you have children, do you have any concerns about their welfare? Nothing tears at the heart of a parent like the sorrow of a child. Someone has said parents are only as happy as their most miserable child. Humanly speaking, this is true.

We must be careful lest we become completely absorbed with our problems. Negative thoughts begin to take over our lives and become the only important facet of life. Such a mindset is evidence of selfishness. We retreat into our cocoon and fail to see other people who need the encouragement of a persevering Christian.

God wants His children living on a different level than the world. We must allow Him to remove our preoccupation with self and see the needs He would have us meet. As we begin to minister, we quickly realize our inadequacy to remedy the problems. The temptation is to become apathetic when viewing the deep needs of people around us. The problems seem utterly overwhelming. Someone has said, "There are no hopeless situations, only people who have grown hopeless about them." *God does not want us to be discouraged about things we cannot do but instead be encouraged by the things He can do.*

Possible With God

"With God all things are possible." (Matthew 19:26c)

The Holy Spirit constantly works with us to bring about a changed way of thinking. As greed's grasp is broken, it is replaced by God's grace and He is able to draw us closer to Himself. At the same time, we begin to see people and things from His perspective. We release God's power to do the impossible when He becomes our reason for living. What happens in the lives of people who relinquish their selfish desires and live to do the Master's will?

- They extend His love.
- Ministry becomes a natural activity.
- Service is not draining.
- They love the unlovable.
- Their relationship to the Lord is sweet.
- Life is an adventure.
- God is able to work miracles.
- They receive blessings.

I mentioned earlier about serving on the committee that was assigned the duty of writing an abstinence-based curriculum and of my discouragement concerning the statistics. Fortunately, the lady who led the group possessed far more faith than I, and she led us in spending endless hours to see the project completed. Every word placed in the curriculum was covered in prayer and eventually it was taught in many schools. God worked through one woman's determination, a host of prayers and the Christian influence of a local Pregnancy Support Center to drastically lower the teenage pregnancy rates in our county. The solution I thought impossible was accomplished by the power of God and the commitment of a few Christians.

Focused on God

God desires to change others through the ministry of His people. However, we are required to have radically changed lives before God can use us effectively. Many Christians are content to live on the fringes of the extraordinary life-never fully experiencing the power of God. Knowing God and doing His will should be our goal in life. Anything less is living the ordinary life. However, when adopting God's mindset, "the things of earth look strangely dim" and life is not the same.

Oswald Chambers says when a person totally surrenders to the Lord, they will never want to go back to the place they were. This is true but it takes spiritual discipline to remain surrendered. We must have the attitude of a good soldier and begin each day focusing on the main duty-following God's commands. However, the things of the world will distract us and we can easily lose our focus.

When I was a child, my grandparents lived a short distance from my home. I often watched as my grandfather began his day's work; although he owned a tractor, he preferred to plow using an old mule. The moment I saw him go to the field with the mule and plow, I ran to meet him. We talked a few minutes and then he began to plow the long rows of corn. I followed for some time and always tried to get his attention.

One day, I could take his inattention no longer. I ran along beside him and yelled as loudly as I could, "Grand Pappy, look at me. Grand Pappy, watch me run. GRAND PAPPY, LOOK AT ME." He never took his eyes off the row of corn and just kept plowing. Finally, when all else failed, I took drastic measures. I picked up a dirt clod, threw it and hit him in the back. I wanted him to stop and talk and he stopped all right! He turned around and I thought trouble was brewing. But he calmly said to me, "Child, you are bothering me; if I look at you and take my eyes off the row, I am going to really tear up things." He returned to his work with a single focus.

My grandfather's focus was on a row of corn and our focus on God should be as consistent. If it is anywhere else, we find our life being torn apart or at the least, ordinary. Each day should begin with a conscious decision to follow the directives of the Holy Spirit. We must put aside those distractions that prevent us from being all God intends us to be. When God is free to work through our lives, He works in ways that are impossible to explain. *Daily living brings daily power if we are daily surrendered to the Lord.*

Greed's Grasp 89

We need to take a heart exam often to determine if the distractions, cares and things of this world have damaged our heart. The damage comes slowly and is the silent killer of our spiritual sensitivity. This condition requires a heart transplant where God places His heart into ours. What would our heart contain if we possessed God's heart? There is a line in a song that says, "God loves people more than anything." This is also the theme of the entire Bible. If we are to have His heart, we must love people more than anything.

The story of David Livingstone is an inspiration to all who have heard of his commitment to the Lord. As a young man, David Livingstone heard a sermon by a missionary to Africa and God captured his heart. God used twenty words from the speaker's address to fire a passion in Livingstone's soul that only death would end. Those words were, "I have sometimes seen, in the morning sun, the smoke of a thousand villages where no missionary has ever been." He determined to be the missionary who would go and share Christ with those who had never heard.

God spoke to Livingstone and said, "Go! Evangelize! Do the work of a missionary! And lo, I am with you, you will never be alone and you will have nothing to fear!" Livingstone staked his life on that call to share the gospel. He went to Africa and won many hearts to the Lord. He suffered numerous attacks of animals, natives, and illnesses.

Livingstone's call to Africa required great sacrifice. He eventually married but his wife was frail and one of his children died in Africa due to harsh living conditions. He felt it would be wrong to risk the lives of his family so, with a sad heart, he sent them back to England. It would be five years of separation as he continued to push deeper into the unknown parts of Africa.

After several years, Livingstone's wife returned to Africa. He was full of joy to have her with him. However, a few weeks later, she became ill and passed away. He buried her under a tree in Africa and wept like a child. He later wrote in his journal the account of this day. He knelt beside her grave, weeping and said, "Oh, Mary, my Mary, I loved you when I married you, and the longer I lived with you, the more I loved you. Now I am left alone and forsaken in the world." But then God spoke to him, "Lo, I am with you." He felt God's presence and strength to continue the work of the Kingdom.

Livingstone traveled 29,000 miles in Africa and shared Christ with everyone who would listen. A journal entry summed up his life, "God had an only son and He was a Missionary. I am a poor imitation, but in this service I hope to live and in it I wish to die. God loved a lost world and gave His only Son to be a Missionary. I love a lost world and I am a missionary, heart and soul. In this service I hope to live and in it I wish to die."

David Livingstone suffered from the ravages of the jungle and early one morning, one of his converts found him dead. He died on his knees beside his bed. As God had promised, he was not alone. As he died, he and God were talking. His body was shipped to England where he was buried in Westminster Abbey. Before his death, he requested his heart be buried in Africa. This was where he had given his life for the Lord and the lost. The Christian natives lovingly opened Livingston's chest, removed his heart and buried it in the African soil.

"Do not lay up for yourselves treasures upon earth, where moth and rust destroy, and where thieves break in and steal. But lay up for yourselves treasures in heaven, where neither moth nor rust destroys, and where thieves do not break in or steal; for where your treasure is, there will your heart be also." (Matthew 6:19-21)

What is your treasure? On what do you spend the majority of your money? Where would they bury your heart if the place was determined by your earthly priorities? Upon what are your eyes focused?

- Clothes
- Shopping
- Interior decorating
- Friends
- Hobby
- Sports
- Your house
- Bank account
- Cars
- Family
- Serving the needy
- Salvation of a lost person

"Turn away my eyes from looking at worthless things." (Psalm 119:37)

Most of us find our priorities are not those of David Livingstone. More importantly, they are not the priorities God desires for us. In light of eternity, most of the things we treasure in this world are worthless. Will your treasures last for eternity? It seems almost impossible to refrain from "keeping up with the Joneses" or to at least continue wanting more and better "things." Most of us have failed in this area during our lives, and we need to seek God's forgiveness. There is good news; God saved us by his grace and by His grace we live. He wants us to fully commit our lives to Him today and then He restructures our priorities through his mercy. Jesus Christ accomplishes impossible things through the person who has undergone a radical heart treatment. When the heart is changed, a changed life follows and God is glorified.

We Have the Cure

The cure for the world's problems is Jesus Christ but what are we doing with the information? Unfortunately, most Christians are doing nothing.

- 91% of the world's population has heard of Coke.
- 74% has seen Coke.
- 51% has tasted Coke.
- 10% of the world's population has heard the gospel.

It is shameful a secular company has accomplished far more in promoting their soft drink than Christians have in proclaiming their Savior. Only a small segment of our world has heard the gospel and the reason is greed among Christians. We spend money on ourselves, we selfishly guard our time and we refuse to give our testimony. We have the cure the world silently begs to know.

Jesus is the answer to the emotional and spiritual needs of each individual. He also offers the opportunity for everyone to have the ultimate healing, eternal life. In Mark 5, the woman sought a cure for her illness; the father urged Jesus to come to the deathbed of his daughter. They realized the solution to their problem was to be found in the Son of God. The solution is the same today, regardless of the situation.

An intimate, obedient relationship with Jesus Christ brings peace that surpasses the problems plaguing mankind. However, many people vainly search for happiness because they do not know the Truth. They find momentary pleasure in illicit sex, drugs and numerous other ways. True happiness eludes them and eventually the pleasure turns to pain.

As a five-year-old child, I adored my brother, Tommy. I followed him wherever he went and was a constant aggravation. One day my dad told him to round up the cows and bring them into the barn. I begged Tommy to let me go with him but he firmly declined my offer. Daddy interceded and I was allowed to accompany him.

Irritated by being forced to oversee his little sister, he decided to end this chore forever. Walking across the field, he pointed to a large bush quite some distance away. He asked, "Do you know what that is?" I replied, "No, what is it?" He said quite emphatically, "That's a feel good bush!" I had never heard of a feel good bush but it sounded interesting. What I didn't know was the bush was actually a prickly ash; it was covered with tiny nettles that sting the skin when touched.

Tommy explained how the bush worked, "I can't believe you have never heard of a feel good bush because it is the most amazing thing. All you have to do is run as fast as you can, jump really high and come down in the middle of the bush on your rear end. The faster you run, the higher you jump, the better it feels. Now Carolyn, I have watched you before and you can really run fast. Now take off, jump high and you will be so happy because of the feel good bush."

I ran with all my might, setting my sights on the promised pleasure. I was kicking up dirt and running faster than the wind. Nearing the bush, my anticipation of the experience grew. I made a flying leap into the air and down I came into thousands of nettles. I had nettles in places I did not even know I had! I started crying and wondered why the feel good bush felt so bad. I was totally ignorant to believe such a tale from my brother.

Many people are falling for a similar lie concerning happiness. The anticipation of fulfillment drives them to participate in activities that are useless at best and harmful at worst. We often think these people are involved in "big sins" like drugs and alcohol. However, happiness can be sought through shopping, entertainment, sports, material possessions, bank accounts and many other ways. Some of these things end in pain and all end in futility.

"I became great and increased more than all who preceded me in Jerusalem. My wisdom also stood by me. All that my eyes desired I did not refuse them. I did not withhold my heart from any pleasure because of my labor and this was my reward for all my labor. Thus I considered all my activities which my hands had done and the labor which I had exerted, and behold all was vanity and striving after wind and there was no profit under the sun." (Ecclesiastes 2:9-11)

Passive Service

Christians are not immune from the temptation of society's lie. They can live wanting the next rush of adrenaline brought about by a new car, bigger house, larger retirement, new furniture, more grandchildren, etc. When the substance of life is summed up in such things, service to the Lord is secondary. A Christian's conscience demands a substitute for total sacrifice.

When Christ is not given first place, attendance and activities at the church often become the measure of Christianity. However, this is passive service. God's Word instructs us to **"not forsake the assembling of ourselves together,"** but that is only our training ground. The actual battle against the sickness of the world begins when we leave the doors of our church.

A young boy was visiting his grandparents and was excited learning about the farm. He was awakened at 5:30 in the morning and told to dress. Coming downstairs and rubbing his eyes, he asked what they were going to do. His grandfather said they were going to feed the animals and a big breakfast awaited them when they were finished. After an hour of feeding pigs, cows and horses, they returned to the house and were greeted by the smell of biscuits, ham and eggs. The little boy ate until he was about to explode, rubbed his stomach and headed upstairs to finish his sleep. The grandfather asked, "Son, where are you going?" The boy replied, "I am going back to sleep, we've worked hard." The wise old man corrected him, "Son, we have only done the chores; the real work is out in the fields."

This is a good description of church attendance and activities. They are important but ministering to the family of God are only the chores. The real work is in the fields, outside the walls of the church. Curing the world's ills will take place only when lay people make Christ a part of their everyday activities. Yet, passive service allows an epidemic of deadly spiritual diseases to flourish. Passive service seldom brings anyone to faith in Jesus and will never bring us joy.

Passionate Sharing

How can we find the purest form of happiness? Joy is found in releasing our *selfish desires* and accepting God's *sacred design* for our lives. God's plan may be unlike anything we would have imagined but it will be interesting and fulfilling.

"Therefore, I urge you, brethren; by the mercies of God to present your bodies a living and holy sacrifice, acceptable to God, which is your spiritual service of worship." (Romans 12:1)

God fills us with Himself as we sacrifice our money, talents, and time. Through His filling, we are prepared to enthusiastically tell what Christ means in our life. We become God's ambassadors by sharing the cure we have experienced. People all around us are suffering a disease without a Savior and it should concern all who know the truth.

In America during the 1950's, summertime was a time of fear and anxiety for many parents; this was the season when children by the thousands were infected with the crippling disease of polio. It became an epidemic and fear escaladed to panic.

My best friend was hospitalized in Murray, Kentucky, suffering the effects of polio. (She eventually recovered with little permanent damage.) My parents did not explain the severity of her condition, only that her legs were stiff because of the disease. As a six-year-old child, I could see the concern on their faces. However, I had no comprehension of the danger to my friend or the fact that polio was highly contagious.

Life for me continued as normal for the next few days. School had started a month earlier and I was having the usual first grade separation difficulties. My greatest problem was being unable to work with my daddy at his tobacco barns. I loved to load my little, red wagon with sawdust and "help" him by unloading it in the barns.

One morning before I got out of bed, I heard my parents talking about my friend's polio and their concern about my exposure to the disease. Mother stated they should go visit the family at the hospital when Daddy finished his work at the barns. Like a stroke of genius, I discovered a way to miss school and work at the barns, all at the same time. I decided I would have a bad case of polio. Descending the steps from my upstairs bedroom, I made lots of noise with my "stiff legs." Walking into the kitchen, I dragged one leg more than the other and watched for their reaction. Fear flooded their faces and I knew things were going my way. Adding a little extra touch, I stiffened my neck and tilted it to one side.

Mother asked how I felt and I weakly dropped my head. Daddy picked me up, carried me to the couch and told me to rest. Relishing the attention, I rolled over and moaned a little. That really got them busy talking! Although they were speaking in hushed tones, I overheard my parents discussing plans to take me to the doctor. Realizing I had only a short time to recover from polio before a doctor's visit, I watched for the school bus. The bus came, honked and pulled away. I had it made!

Before leaving for the doctor's office, daddy hurriedly left to check the fires in the barn. Hearing the door shut, I jumped off the couch, dressed quickly and headed outside. At the same time, my mother was looking out the window and praying her little girl would not forever be lame from this dreaded disease. The sight from the window made her both angry and relieved. She saw me run across the back yard, jump a small stump, grab my little, red wagon and scurry to the barn. NO LIMPING!

Following me to the barn, she talked with my dad and somehow I knew I no longer "had it made." Their worry turned into wondering how best to discipline me for the terrible scare I had given them. They gave the worst discipline a child can experience; both cried and said how I had hurt them. Of course, I started crying also. The discipline continued when I had to leave my little, red wagon at the barn and they took me to school. I cried all the way and they loved it so!

My experience with polio was fake and selfishly driven. However, many children died from the disease and thousands more were left crippled for life. During this epidemic, Jonas Salk searched for a cure. His discovery of a vaccination using a "killed" virus led to one of the most dramatic breakthroughs in the history of medicine. The fear of polio was lifted when it was announced Salk had developed a vaccine against the disease. He never patented his polio vaccine, but distributed the formula freely, so the whole world could benefit from his discovery. Jonas Salk could have:

- Been afraid to share the cure.
- Continued in med school until he knew more.
- Feared some would refuse the cure.
- Remained silent due to unconcern.

How do we handle the cure we have experienced in Christ? Are we afraid of sharing; continue attendance in church year after year until we learn more about ministry and witnessing; refuse to give the cure because someone might reject us; remain silent due to unconcern? We can emulate Jonas Salk and freely distribute the hope of Jesus Christ to the hurting people of the world. Are we apathetic and greedy with our resources or are we passionate about sharing?

I mentioned earlier in the book my daughter's struggle with infertility. As with anyone who desires something very deeply, she became almost desperate for a child. Her desperation turned to joy as baby Luke was placed in her arms. The gratitude toward Luke's birth mother was overflowing. Jenise wrote the following letter to Luke's birth mother the morning they brought him home from the hospital.

I will thank God daily for the blessing of Luke and you for this precious gift.

Dear _____,
Today is a memorable day for both of us-you and me. It is with both joy and sadness that we both feel affected by the tiniest of creatures. There is no way I can adequately thank you for the opportunity to be a mother. This is a day I have always dreamed of since I was a child and for the past six years thought would never happen. You are a special lady and I will always keep

a spot in my heart for you and your unselfishness. As for precious Luke, he will be and already is very loved. Because of you, I am forever a changed woman-I am a Mother.

With Awesome Gratitude,

Jenise

As Jenise desperately desired to have a child, we must desperately desire to bear spiritual children. Oh that we could have the passionate hearts of Peter and John, desperately desiring to tell of Jesus.

"And when they had summoned them, they commanded them not to speak or teach at all in the name of Jesus. But Peter and John answered and said to them, "Whether it is right in the sight of God to give heed to you rather than to God, you be the judge; for we cannot stop speaking what we have seen and heard." (Acts 4:18-20)

How passionate are you about God's calling on your life?

- Desperately desiring to bear spiritual children?
- Desperately desiring to know God and His will for your life?
- Desperately desiring to be obedient regardless of the cost?
- Desperately desiring for God to change your lifestyle so others will know Him?
- Desperately desiring to live the supernatural, extraordinary life?

God takes control when greed's grasp is broken; you find the ordinary life melting away and a transformed life taking hold. The result is overflowing gratitude for the One who loves you, gave Himself for you and changed your priorities. Out of gratitude, you can say, "I am forever a changed person-I am completely Yours."

"Not that I speak from want, for I have learned to be content in whatever circumstances I am. I know how to live in prosperity; in any and every circumstance I have learned the secret of being filled and going hungry, both of having abundance and suffering need. I can do all things through Him who strengthens me." (Philippians 4:11-13)

Chapter 4

Religious Retreat

"You shall love your neighbor as yourself."
Matthew 22:39b

Section 1

Me, a Minister?

When my daughter, Michelle, was in college, she spent a weekend at my house and delayed her departure until dusky dark on Sunday afternoon. With a ninety-mile trip back to Chattanooga, she chose a state road rather than the interstate to save time. Not long into the trip, a deer ran out of the woods adjacent to the highway and grazed the back of her car. A city girl, Michelle had not seen a live deer up close, much less been involved in an accident with one. Shaken but unhurt, she steered the car to the shoulder of the road and got out to inspect for damage.

The reader needs a mental picture of this scene. Here is a twenty-one-year-old coed with long blond hair, big brown eyes, athletic figure, driving a small, white sporty-looking Honda. She was wandering on foot next to the highway. Later that night, she called to let me know she was back at school and began describing her experience, "Momma, you wouldn't believe it. By the time I got out of the car, four or five pick-up trucks had stopped." "Really," I responded. "And all the drivers were male, right?" "How did you know?" she marveled. "Oh, just a wild guess," I said. Michelle continued, "They were so nice, Momma. They walked around my car with me to check for damage, and there wasn't any. Then they offered to take me anywhere I wanted to go." "You didn't leave with any of them, did you?" I worriedly asked. "No, of course not," she responded, "but they were so sweet and helpful. I didn't know people could be so great!"

A few months later on the same state highway, Carolyn and I were returning from a day's work at my rental property. It was late afternoon in July, and the temperature was close to one hundred degrees. My car suddenly quit; nothing electrical was working, including the power steering. Carolyn was driving and carefully guided the car onto the shoulder of the road. We speculated it was the alternator since the air conditioner was not working either. I had a cell phone, called a tow truck, and prepared for at least a thirty-minute wait in the heat. We got out of the car and stood on the side of the road for several minutes. Traffic on the road was brisk and many vehicles passed us. No one stopped, male or female. Finally, the lady who lived in a nearby house came by and offered us a drink of water. Still no vehicles stopped to help us.

After we began to sweat profusely, I noticed a shady area across the highway and suggested we cross over and stand on that side. Traffic continued to be brisk; still no offers of assistance. While we were waiting, I noticed a bad smell where we were standing. The longer we stood, the worse it smelled. Because Carolyn grew up on a farm, I consider her an expert on all matters outdoors, so I asked, "What is that stench? I've never smelled anything quite as awful!" She looked at me with eyes of utter seriousness and responded, "Ann, that is where old women have had car trouble on this road. They have stood here until they died; then they come and roll them down the hill. That's what you are smelling!" It took me several seconds to realize she was kidding because I felt like I might die where I stood.

I learned that day people pick and choose, based on appearances, whom they will stop and help; the older you are, the less likely you are to attract assistance. Christians should minister to a need no matter what the age or station of the recipient; often that is not the case. Going-to-meeting-church members think of themselves as compassionate, good-hearted, and loving. However, some of the most narrow-minded, inflexible, and judgmental people are found in the ranks of the religious. Sadly, in some cases, non-Christians find more fellowship and understanding at the clubs and bars than they do from Christian relatives and friends. In short, many of us have retreated to the pew to be insulated from the sinful, needy society surrounding us. We have a sanitized church, distanced from the world and its values, and within its walls we find the opportunity to pick and choose our ministries. Some church members choose *not* to minister while others participate in clean, acceptable ministries with attractive recipients.

Religious retreat is another barrier to the extraordinary life God would choose for us. Hyper-religious people often settle for the goodness found in ritualistic behavior, and their satisfaction comes from self-chosen works. Often, "good works" are reserved for fellow members within the church congregation. Some of God's greatest blessings are found outside the religious perimeter. Unfortunately, we miss them because of our spiritual insulation.

Several years ago, our Sunday school class spearheaded a mission's emphasis to the Appalachia area of upper East Tennessee. During our second summer of ministry, I discovered some of God's blessings come in dirty containers. We were assigned by the on-site mission coordinator to renovate the home of an elderly woman named Babe. Babe had been forced out of her house and taken to North Carolina to work for relatives, and her home remained vacant during her absence. Someone kicked in the door and packs of dogs and stray cats roamed in and out of the structure. Adding to the filth and destruction was a roof leak. With no money to clean and repair it, Babe was forced to move into the squalid house when she returned. For a while, Babe continued to allow the stray dogs and cats to cohabit the house. She became quite ill, was hospitalized, and health officials told her the animals had to leave or she could not go home. She agreed to their demands but kept one cat, which was mangy and flea-infested.

Arriving that summer, we found a suspicious, unhappy Babe and an odor that would knock you down at the door. At first, we doubted our team could stand working inside because there were dried animal droppings under beds, chairs, and couches. An ammonia-like smell permeated everything; our nostrils stung and stomachs turned, as we entered the front door. Babe adamantly resisted our suggestion to open the windows. Finally, the construction leader asked Carolyn and me to distract her while they opened the windows and set up fans for ventilation. Our assignment for the week was to sit with Babe, take her on errands in the car, and fellowship with her to alleviate her fears while the construction team worked in her home.

As the week progressed, we fell in love with Babe as she did with us. The guys on site told us as soon as Carolyn and I pulled out of her driveway, Babe would light up a cigarette; she never smoked in front of us. Every night when we returned to the hotel, our smelly clothes had to be placed in another location until they could be laundered. For some reason, mosquitoes and fleas love me, and I had over two hundred fleabites on my body during that week. Despite the adverse working conditions, God blessed us with a wonderful friendship. The fearful, suspicious Babe was gone by the end of the week. A new lady with a fresh perm and a big smile hugged and covered us with toothless kisses when we left. We embraced and cried, grateful the odor of neglect and abuse had been replaced with the sweet aroma of the Spirit. We had completely refurbished the house, every wall washed, new carpet, ceiling tile and appliances. Such are the blessings when God chooses the ministry.

Indeed, there are lost and hurting individuals in every town and city. Carolyn and I live in Rutherford County, Tennessee, where in the past thirty years there has been a remarkable turnaround in church attendance. In the early 1970's approximately 75% of the population was found inside a church building on Sunday morning. In 2006, on any given Sunday, only 25% of our county makes its way to a house of worship. *Simply stated, the people who need us the most are found outside the religious fellowships we attend.*

I heard this illustration several years ago related by pastor James Merritt. Before the days of electricity, a young farmer and his wife were expecting their first child. Late one evening the young woman went into labor, and the farmer sent for the doctor. When he arrived, the doctor gave orders for the husband to boil water and gather fresh towels. The wife began hard labor, and the physician instructed the farmer to hold the lantern to provide light for the delivery. Soon a baby girl was born. "Congratulations," remarked the doctor, "you have a daughter." The relieved farmer began cleaning the child when his wife suddenly went into hard labor again. "Hurry, bring the lantern, hold it for me," requested the doctor. In a few more minutes another baby was delivered. "Congratulations, young man, you are the father of a son!" Well, the farmer was extremely excited at the prospects of a boy. He returned to cleaning the babies when, to his dismay, the wife went into labor once more. "Bring the lantern again," barked the doctor. At this point the farmer's excitement was gone, replaced by fear. "Do you think the light's drawing um, doc?"

The purpose of ministry is to present the light of the gospel to a lost and hurting world to draw them to our Savior. Christ's plan for our lives cannot be confined to church attendance, committee meetings and Sunday dinners. By limiting ministry to those in our church ranks, we miss the adventure of an extraordinary life of new relationships. Many have chosen religious retreat rather than engage in spiritual warfare. While we are content to speak up on moral issues, many times judgmentally, society is waiting for us to exhibit the love of Christ in tangible ways.

Christ confronted the issue of religiosity in a familiar New Testament passage entitled *The Good Samaritan*. The relating of the story was precipitated by a question from a staunch member of the religious establishment.

"And a lawyer stood up and put Him to the test, saying, 'Teacher, what shall I do to inherit eternal life?'" (Luke 10:25)

We must remember people who would not consider attending church may show interest in avoiding death and living forever. Lost people are curious, afraid, and willing to talk about issues that affect them where they are. Jesus engaged this religious but lost gentleman in a conversation, which resulted in one of the most powerful stories in the Bible. After the lawyer recited a portion of the Ten Commandments, Jesus commended him.

"But wishing to justify himself, he said to Jesus, 'And who is my neighbor?'" (Luke 10:29)

The lawyer had the letter of the law but not the spirit of the law. Religion-only people seek to justify themselves by their good works. *The man thought he could pick his good works by choosing the recipients.* Likewise, we find ways to justify ourselves before God with good works like church committee memberships, worship attendance, choir rehearsals, and monetary contributions. Jesus responded to the question with a story in which every reader can find himself represented. Each character is a type of person found in our society. Where do you find yourself?

Senseless Tragedy

The Victim

"Jesus replied and said, 'A man was going down from Jerusalem to Jericho and fell among robbers, and they stripped him and beat him, and went away leaving him half dead.'" (Luke 10:30)

Little detail is given about the victim in this story. We can assume he was a real man, not a fictionalized character, since Jesus tells the story as fact, not parable. He was more than likely a Jew since the Samaritan is quickly identified by race when he is introduced to the story. We also know he was a foolish man. In these times, traveling alone from Jerusalem to Jericho with goods worth stealing was too dangerous to attempt. Thieves and murderers hid in the rocks and cliffs surrounding this treacherous road, and prudent travelers and merchants chose to join a caravan. Only the foolish would make such a trip alone.

Many tragic and adverse situations have been brought on by poor decisions and lifestyle choices. While all of us have made faulty decisions, Christians looking for a reason to avoid ministry can often find evidence, rightly or wrongly, to blame the victim for his dilemma. Nowhere in Scripture do we find Jesus questioning the causes before He sought to minister to the need. In fact, He urges ministry to "the least of these," indicating there are those who in no way deserve our help. If we examine our own lives, there is little within us worthy of God's mercy. The essence of grace is that God reaches down to us when we least deserve it. He asks us to do the same for the hurting people who surround us.

You may feel like the victim in this story. When spouses walk out to enter an adulterous relationship, there are wounds, anger, and feelings of abandonment. When partners or employees steal and leave the owner of the business to pay the bills, the injured party feels beaten, foolish, and forsaken. On the other hand, you may have purposely, with eyes wide open, chosen the circumstances wounding your spirit. For those who were raised as children of alcoholics, in drug-addicted situations, or victims of abuse, there is an undefined, smoldering pain that is forever present. Such children are victims, and they take their wounds into adult relationships.

God does not want us to judge behavior; He wants us to gently minister. During the throes of my family breakup, I was amazed at the people who called, encouraged, and helped me. I was also amazed by the people who did not. Some friends later shared with me they did not know how to deal with my emotional pain. Not knowing what to do or say, they walked away from the friendship. More than once, I told Carolyn the hardest place to go during the week was church. I looked forward to Monday morning because I found the people at work far less judgmental, more encouraging, and much more inclusive. It is sad the church family often gives more criticism than compassion.

If you find yourself the victim of circumstances you created or a situation over which you had little or no control, be encouraged. God loves you. He is watching over your life and will send the help you need, when you need it. Depend on Him. There was a period of time during the legal proceedings surrounding our divorce that I was forced to live every other week in an apartment. My husband stayed with the children on alternate weeks, and I had to move out and live elsewhere. This arrangement continued for approximately four months, and I absolutely hit bottom emotionally during this time. I could not bear spending half the time away from my children.

One night, I was so low I climbed into bed around 7:00 and challenged the Lord, "If I ever get up again, You will have to get me up. I am finished." I soaked my pillow with tears and wallowed in the misery of it. After running dry from crying, I tried fitful prayers and then sleep. About an hour later, my phone rang; on the other end of the line was a minister/friend in a distant city. I had done some work for him in the past, and he called to check on me. Immediately recognizing the depth of my depression, he allowed me to talk as he encouraged and comforted. An hour later, we hung up, and I jumped out of bed and started doing laundry. Within a few minutes, I remembered my challenge to the Lord, "If I ever get up again, You will have to do it." Sure enough, He did. I am grateful one of His servants was obedient and telephoned me.

If everything is fine in your life presently, then rejoice. Turn and help someone who is hurting because your time of need will come. It is inevitable the situations of life will wound you at some point. A friend of mine shared at one time she was happily married to a professional man. They were church attendees, financially successful, and happy. She would look at people going through marital problems and quite judgmentally think, "Why can't they figure life out? It's really not that hard. I wish they would get it together." A few years later, after the birth of a child, her husband walked out and filed for divorce. She said, "Suddenly, I understood that life was hard. I didn't have it all together any more. Things were not as easy as I once thought." She had become the victim.

Steeped in Religion

The Priest and the Levite

Jesus introduces two more characters in this intriguing story: the priest and the Levite. These men represent the religious establishment of the day. They are Jews, strong upholders of the Law, and well respected.

> **"And by chance a priest was going down on that road, and when he saw him, he passed by on the other side. Likewise, a Levite also, when he came to the place and saw him, passed by on the other side." (Luke 10:31-32)**

They are good men with bad hearts; they can see pain and turn their heads. They represent the religious figures of our day as well. It is easy for us to reflect them into the roles of pastor and deacon, but they could be a Sunday school teacher, choir member, or any respected church member. When Christians are confronted with human need and ignore it, they represent the priest or the Levite.

Yes, they had reasons for continuing their trip without stopping. The priest was unsure if the wounded man was dead or alive. If he touched a dead body, the priest would be ceremonially unclean and unable to participate in temple worship. The Levite may have been afraid for his safety. Often thieves would use a prostrate man as a decoy. As soon as the passerby knelt to look, the thieves would jump from the rocks and attack. Pressing responsibilities and prudence can provide excuses to avoid ministry in any needy situation.

When my children were preschool age, several young mothers in our church organized a coffee break fellowship at our church each Tuesday morning. People who worked in the downtown area, other mothers, the elderly, and anyone interested were invited to drop in for a few minutes for coffee, soft drinks, and snacks. We had a good response, and the event continued for several months. There was a halfway house for mentally disturbed patients a block away from the church, and a lady from the home began attending the coffee break and church services. She was old enough to be my mother and had multiple needs, personally and emotionally. She began to ask us to go on shopping trips and for other favors. We approached a staff member to see if we could organize a ministry for the residents at the halfway house. I will never forget his words, "You are young mothers. Your first responsibility is to your children. You can do some kind of ministry when you're older and your children are raised." The idea was dropped for lack of support, but I was haunted by this staff member's words. Somehow, I sensed spiritually this attitude was not of God. Pressing responsibilities are not an excuse to turn away from human need.

Many of us have confused the meaning of the word "good." We measure our goodness in terms of church attendance rather than attending to human need. I taught a ladies' Sunday school class for years. Early one Sunday morning I received a phone call from one of my most faithful members. Her best friend, also a member of our church, was dying with cancer; doctors gave her only a few weeks to live. She wanted some advice. Would it be okay for her to miss Sunday school to sit with her dying friend? I sensed her desire was to be with her friend, but it broke my heart she needed my permission to miss church. *What kind of religion promotes ritual as righteousness?* I certainly do not want to be a part of a works-based religion; unfortunately, sometimes I practice self-righteousness.

Carolyn and I exercise every morning we can. Several years ago, we went to the local shopping mall to walk during extremely cold weather. One particular morning, we planned to walk, return home for showers, and travel to a local assisted living facility to teach a Bible study. We had allotted just enough time to do all three. After a couple of trips around the mall, I looked toward the front entrance and saw a woman lying on the floor with a security guard standing over her. Calling Carolyn's attention to the sight, she wondered out loud if we should approach the woman and determine the problem. My response? "We are running short on time. Since someone is with her, let's make another trip around the mall. If she's still lying there when we get back, then we'll check." I am not proud of the response, but that is what I said.

We made another lap, and when we approached the door, the woman was still on the floor. Quite a crowd had gathered, and an ambulance was approaching the front entrance. This time Carolyn took matters into her own hands, threaded us through the crowd, and knelt down on the floor. "Would you like for us to go with you to the hospital?" "Yes," the young woman responded. "We will meet you there," Carolyn assured her.

As we headed to the car, I was looking at my watch, still fretting. "We don't have much time. The Bible study is at 11:00; I hope we can make it." Again, I am not proud of my response, but religious responsibility was primary in my mind. However, God was in control. As we entered the

ER waiting room, the elderly volunteer behind the greeter's desk was a member of our church. He immediately took us to the examining room where the young woman was lying. We inquired about her need, and she asked us to go get her sister. Fortunately, the sister and her husband lived two blocks from the hospital, and we returned with them in a matter of fifteen minutes. At that point, the woman was satisfied with the companionship of her family; we were able to leave. We promised to pray for her and gave her our telephone numbers to call if she needed us in any way.

We made it to our Bible study on time that day. I am not sure if I had time to wash my hair, but it did not matter. God had ordered our day to meet every need He placed in our path. When our eyes are on moral goodness, we are self-focused. This attitude will do little to draw people to Christ, and it will suffocate our spiritual growth. Attend to the need God has placed before you; He will take care of the details and schedule your day.

Stopped by Compassion

The Samaritan

"But a Samaritan, who was on a journey, came upon him; and when he saw him, he felt compassion." (Luke 10:33)

The Samaritan was immediately identified by his race for a reason. The Jews and Samaritans felt great animosity toward each other. Jews regarded Samaritans as half-breeds and would go miles out of their way to avoid contact with one. It had to infuriate Jesus' audience of legalistic Jews for a Samaritan to be introduced as the hero of His story. Jesus was making the focus of the story the condition of the heart rather than the color of the skin. His point would be made but not well taken.

Notice the overwhelming emotion felt by the Samaritan man–compassion. I ran across a definition of compassion that grabbed my heart. Compassion is mercy to the depth of one's being. Compassion is an emotion, but it is also a spiritual gift called mercy. Not everyone has the gift of compassion, but it can be learned. Carolyn is gifted with mercy, and I have become more sensitive to human needs and emotions by being around her. At first, though, I was quite skeptical about mercy's value.

Our pastor preached a sermon several years ago on spiritual gifts. He took the situation of a boy crashing a bicycle and used it as an illustration of how people with differing spiritual gifts would react.

Someone with the gift of giving might approach the crying child with the reassurance he would buy him a replacement bicycle. Someone with the gift of teaching would ask the child what lesson he learned from the crash–how to prevent another bicycle wreck. However, someone with the gift of mercy would sit down on the ground next to the child and cry with him. I punched Carolyn and whispered, "See how useless that is. Now you have two crying people instead of one." Carolyn responded, "It's useless unless you are the little boy." Immediately, I saw her point. Compassion is the ability to place oneself in the other's shoes, to feel and experience the same pain.

Notice also in this verse, we are told the Samaritan is on a journey in comparison to the priest and Levite who were just "going by." The Samaritan had a lot more to lose by stopping. He had a long journey, and by tending a wounded man, much time would be lost. Smug, self-righteous people are never on a journey; they are just "passing by." I was reminded recently of how hypocritical Christians can be in their dealings with those outside the church. My son and daughter-in-law, Lauren, moved to Chattanooga and purchased a home. The realtor told them the neighbors to their left were missionaries living out of the country and were rarely home. The previous homeowner regularly parked in their driveway when she had company. Arriving in Chattanooga to help my son repaint the house, I parked in the neighboring driveway, rather than block their cars.

All went well until late afternoon. My son looked out the window and said, "Someone is pulling into the driveway next door." Lauren called to the bedroom where we were painting and said, "I think we are going to meet our neighbors." She walked to the back door, smiled, and said, "Hi, I'm." Before she could say another word, a scowling older man barked, "You need to move your car right now!" He then turned, went back to his vehicle, and Lauren walked to the bedroom in tears. Rad grabbed the car keys, moved my car, and tried to engage the neighbors in conversation. He learned this couple was not the homeowner but friends who used the house when they were in the area. They, too, were traveling missionaries whose ministry extended no more than a day's journey from Chattanooga. Rad said the woman was somewhat friendly, but her husband remained unpleasant, even after Rad apologized for blocking the driveway. Keep in mind this was Rad and Lauren's first day in the neighborhood. I asked myself, "What good is this couple's traveling over the state of Tennessee to minister when they cannot be friendly to the new, young couple next door? For all they knew, my son and daughter-in-law might not be Christians. If they had been lost, what would they have thought of two missionaries who would not introduce themselves before gruffly demanding they move a car?

In contrast, the Samaritan felt compassion for the injured man at first glance. His immediate mercy proves circumstances do not determine reaction. All three men gazed on the same circumstance but there were two distinctly different reactions. There is not enough suffering in the world to elicit compassion. Compassion is a heart condition that must spring first from the heart of God. To teach mercy, God will place people in situations that require it.

In 1986, Carolyn and I were a part of a mission team from our state denomination that led a series of conferences in Michigan. Six women were on the team, and we led age-level conferences in various churches across the state. We traveled all week in a van; on our last night, we were speeding to the church where our conferences would be held. Unfamiliar with the area, we were running late. Carolyn was riding in the front, serving as navigator, and I was sitting in the back seat with another member of our team.

Suddenly, I heard someone outside the van screaming. I thought, "That is so rude to have someone in the yard yelling at a pet or child." I looked to my right and saw an elderly woman lying on her front stoop. She was yelling, "Help me, somebody, please help me!" The lady next to me and I both screamed at the same time for the driver to stop the van, and we pointed to the elderly woman. Carolyn, the other team member, and I jumped out of the van, ran across a busy intersection, and descended on the house. Carolyn raced into the home to call 911 but could not locate the phone. The house was a complete wreck, garbage, empty beer cans, and clutter everywhere. She finally stopped and prayed for God to show her the phone and she called for an ambulance.

We searched for a blanket to cover the lady because it was October and quite cool. The woman was abnormally blue, more than the temperature would cause. Carolyn knelt on the stoop and held her while we waited. The neighbors walked over but maintained a safe distance from the scene. We learned from them the woman's name was Roberta, and she had recently been hospitalized. She continued to cry, "Help me. Help me, God. Please help me." We reassured her she would be okay and we were praying for her. A few minutes later the ambulance arrived.

Shaken and quite late, we proceeded to the church and led our conferences. However, we learned later Miss Roberta died on the way to the hospital from a blood clot that had entered her lungs. I could not get her last words to leave my head. "God, please help me." After returning home, I continued to visualize those last moments of her life. I prayed and asked God what it all meant. Days went by before He spoke. Quietly, one night in my prayer time, God answered and softly said, "I have shown you a picture of a lost and dying world on judgment day." I knew then my neighbors, friends, and associates would be calling out for salvation on that day, but it would be too late. The time to evangelize is now. I want to have a heart for lost people, the heart of God, one of compassion. I want to be the Good Samaritan–a pilgrim on a journey of mercy.

Stored Up for Ministry

"And he came to him and bandaged up his wounds, pouring oil and wine on them; and he put him on his own beast, and brought him to an inn and took care of him." (Luke 10:34)

God uses prepared people. That may sound trite, but the Good Samaritan proves the adage. He not only gave of his time, he had supplies with him to minister to the man's wounds. My children knew the resources available in my purse when they encountered trouble. Mom had band-aids, pain relievers, motion-sickness pills, tissues, and small change for emergencies. The younger generation carries debit cards, but older mothers still have dollar bills for parking and small purchases. Even though they are grown, my children still expect me to provide tissues, comfort, and small change when we are together. God asks Christians to have a parent's heart and be prepared for ministry to a needy world.

My former pastor shared when he was a young college student desiring to enter seminary, he and a friend would hitchhike from Knoxville to Carson-Newman College to attend classes. As they walked, the two friends would lament the few invitations they were receiving to preach. They desperately desired the experience of preaching before a church congregation. One day, an older pastor picked them up on the road and transported them to Jefferson City. While they traveled, the young men were complaining about the lack of preaching. The older pastor asked them, "Boys, how many sermons have you prepared?" Both men hung their heads in embarrassment because they had not prepared even one sermon. The older man laughed and said, "Get yourself some sermons, then God will use you."

Prayer

Prayer is the first step in preparation for ministry. I would suspect the Samaritan man *actually liked* ministry; he may have prayed that morning for God to give him an opportunity to help someone. When was the last time you prayed God would intersect your life with someone you could help? I remember praying for such an opportunity one day as Carolyn and I began our daily walk on the wilderness trail near our homes. I felt God tug at my heart, "Today I have someone who needs you." We walked to the end of the trail and turned around to return to our cars. We were still fifteen minutes away from the edge of the park when a young woman approached us from the opposite direction. Her face was red from the heat, her breathing was labored, and she appeared distraught. She grabbed Carolyn and hugged her, and we realized she was afflicted with Down syndrome and was lost. As we began to question her, we discovered she was so profoundly affected she could not speak. The young woman locked her arm around Carolyn's waist, refusing to turn loose, and we resumed our walk toward the park's edge. She was extremely hot; we were concerned she could not finish the walk. My mind raced with possibilities:

- What if we could not find her family?
- What if she collapsed?
- Was there enough cell signal to call for help?
- Did she have heart problems?

Every person we passed on the trail, we expected a cry of joy her child had been found; yet, everyone looked at us blankly. Finally, we reached a fork in the path, and our anxiety increased. The scared, young woman could not tell us which way her companions had gone. Like a toddler, though, her body language guided us as she pulled to the left. This particular fork in the trail led to the river and would take us farther away from help. Were we doing the right thing to follow her directions? Again, the people passing us looked at the young woman with no recognition, and she continued to pant and grip Carolyn tighter.

Suddenly, the path ended at the river; and as we looked down to the shore, a group of handicapped hikers was standing on the river's edge with their sponsors. Our companion was elated when she saw her friends. I climbed down the embankment to talk with the leader. I learned our new friend's name was Diane, and her absence had just been discovered. I registered our fears about Diane's well being and the leaders' need to keep a better accounting of the group. We made sure she was feeling better before we left. As we walked to our cars, I knew God had used us; but He had prepared us through prayer, placing within us a desire to help.

God-given ability

In addition to spiritual willingness, the Samaritan man was prepared with ability. While not all of us can minister medically, each person is trained or can be trained to do something. We have a friend in her early eighties. Every summer she travels to East Tennessee and cooks for campers and summer missionaries at a Christian camp. The first few years, she slept on a cot with no air-conditioning. The camp leaders recently air-conditioned her room, and she has organized several more volunteers to go with her. This lady loves to cook for family and friends and has turned her ability into a ministry. God has equipped you with a talent or gift He desires to use in meeting needs. If God directs you to a new, complex ministry, be willing to take training because God uses prepared people!

Money and resources

"On the next day he took out two denarii and gave them to the innkeeper and said, 'Take care of him; and whatever more you spend, when I return, I will repay you.'" (Luke 10:35)

In addition to prayer and ability, money and resources are needed in ministry. The Samaritan man did not hesitate to place the injured victim on his own beast and pay for his room and board at the inn. Many Christians are so strapped for money they would be hard pressed to help another. Carolyn and I have some friends who years ago opened a separate bank account and named it "God's account." They place extra money they have earned and do not need or unexpected windfalls into the account. Then when a need is brought to their attention, they have funds to meet it. Of course, to establish a God's account, there must be a commitment to live below a family's means rather than beyond its means. The Good Samaritan's agenda includes time, talents, possessions, and cash. Such a lifestyle is in stark contrast to our culture and carnal nature.

In addition to personal ministry, I find in the *Good Samaritan* story a time for professional ministry to individuals. Through a family crisis in 1984, God revealed an aspect of the scripture to me I had never seen. For a period of two weeks, I had continuously turned into Luke chapter ten during my Bible study and quiet time. At one point I checked to see if I had placed a bookmark in my Bible because I turned there every day and read it. It was not coincidence, but I did not know why God continually drew my attention to the passage.

It was the fall of the year, and my mother had been experiencing extreme bouts of depression. One afternoon, my brother called and said I needed to travel to my parent's house, four hundred miles away, as quickly as possible. Mother had grown significantly worse. My father and grandmother were with my mother, but they did not know what to do for her. My brother and sister were also making plans to come home. I was the first child to arrive and was shocked at mother's deterioration. When my siblings arrived, all three of us attempted to talk mother into a voluntary commitment to a mental hospital; she refused. The next day, as we were planning to leave, mother finally consented to go. We all accompanied her to the hospital.

I have been through some difficult situations in my lifetime, but this was one of the hardest things I have ever done. Every door was locked. It was unlocked long enough for us to pass through, and then relocked. Once mom was admitted, we could have no communication with her for two weeks. When we left, I felt as if we had abandoned her.

My brother and I rode to the airport together and boarded a plane for Atlanta. I was shaken to the core and weeping. After the plane took off, I opened my Bible to Luke 10:30-37. As I reread this familiar passage, the words of verse 35 jumped off the page.

"On the next day he took out two denarii and gave them to the innkeeper and said, 'Take care of him...'"

The Lord quietly spoke, "Ann, you did the right thing." At that moment I knew mother was exactly where she needed to be–in the care of professionals. I had entrusted her to someone else, and it was right. God's Word proved to be my comfort in a difficult time.

You may be in a similar situation. A loved one or friend may desperately need more than personal ministry. It may be time to suggest and research professional help. Alcoholism, drug addiction, eating disorders, sexual perversion, depression, and other psychiatric problems may require more than love and personal ministry. While the loving touch of a friend or relative is primary and needed, the healing touch of a trained professional should not to be ignored. Do not be ashamed to seek advice. God has equipped people with education and experience to provide help. Their resources may be God's resources for your need or the needs of your friend or relative.

"'Which of these three do you think proved to be a neighbor to the man who fell into the robbers' hands?' And he said, 'The one who showed mercy toward him.' Then Jesus said to him, 'Go and do the same.'" (Luke 10:35-36)

Jesus completes his story and brings the conversation back to the lawyer's original question, "And who is my neighbor?" As a master communicator and teacher, He challenges the man to answer the question himself, based upon the story. The lawyer could not bring himself to utter the word *Samaritan*, so he identifies the man who proved to be a neighbor as "the one who showed mercy." He answered the question for all time. My neighbor is anyone around me with a need.

To live the extraordinary life of faith, God asks us to abandon religious retreat and self-constructed isolation. Step boldly into the relationships God has designed for your life as you lovingly meet the needs of others. The world is not interested in opinions as much as actions. Enter into His ministry of mercy and love.

"For just as the body without the spirit is dead, so also faith without works is dead." (James 2:26)

Section 2

My God-Given Responsibility

As a child I had the privilege of growing up on a farm; there was little to do except work. Formal recreation was an unknown event, so I sometimes experienced boredom. Therefore, it became the responsibility for those of us who lived in rural West Tennessee to envision ways to occupy the small amount of available free time.

Sunday was one of those times and special in the life of my family. There was never a question as to whether we were going to church; it was an accepted fact. The country church I attended was only a short distance from my house and was an integral part of my existence. My parents were devout Christians and they diligently taught me at an early age to respect the church building. I tried to live out their expectations, especially since I knew the consequences of disrespect.

After church each Sunday, I would go to a friend's house or she would come to mine. My sister had the same arrangement with her friend and we would search for ways to entertain the visitors when they came to our home. After lunch, we often sneaked to church, telling our parents we were going out to play. Although we knew the strict rules concerning respect for the church building, we could not resist having our own Sunday afternoon worship services.

My sister led the singing, her friend played the piano, my friend was the audience and I preached. Our services were very lengthy, and although my preaching lacked substance and theology, I always found something to say. (I was approximately eight years old.) My friend, the audience, would often go to sleep as is common in most worship services! Not to be deterred, I preached on and on until my sister told me to shut up!

Our favorite time was when a baptismal service was scheduled for Sunday nights at the church, which meant the baptistery was filled with water on Sunday afternoons. Arriving at the church, we proceeded with the regular song service; my sister leading the singing, her friend at the piano. Following the singing, we solemnly entered the time for baptisms. Since I was the preacher, it was my responsibility to conduct the service, but we only had one candidate, my friend. Since we delighted in long services, it seemed a shame to baptize only one person. Therefore, we instructed her after the baptism, she was to circle around and return to be baptized again. This ritual went on and on until I was exhausted or my sister told me to shut up and get out of the water. Certainly, if water baptism could get someone to heaven, my friend would be thoroughly qualified!

We all had a great time playing church, even though we knew the consequences if our parents ever learned of the antics. Fortunately for us, they never discovered our activities and we survived. However, many Christians are guilty of playing church and seem unaware of the consequences. We go to worship activities but the Spirit of God does not energize our lives. We lack the salt and light that brings change. Going through the motions of worship, we disrespect the One who died so lives might be fully transformed. Honestly ask yourself, "Am I playing church or am I pleasing Christ?"

"You were formerly darkness but now you are Light in the Lord, walk as children of Light (for the fruit of the Light consists in all goodness and righteousness and truth), trying to learn what is pleasing to the Lord." (Ephesians 5:8-10)

We have the God-given responsibility to allow God's light to shine through us and, therefore, be His witnesses at all times. *Rituals and religious activities will not enable us to burn brightly enough for others to see Christ.* The Light can break through the darkness as we cease playing church and begin pleasing God through radical obedience.

Ann shared earlier in the chapter about Diane, the young woman with Down syndrome. She was lost, at a crossroad, and unsure which path to take. Today, all of us are at a crossroad and we have a choice to make. One road seems safe, secure and familiar. It is the easy way because we have traveled it for years. The other road is different; only God knows the twists and turns. The interruptions along the way can be extremely challenging. This is a departure from the known and requires trust; a total commitment to following God's directions. This road holds opportunities to minister in Jesus' name but the trip may seem perilous at times. However, strength for the journey is assured and joy awaits you daily. We chose each day which road to travel and our blessings depend upon our choices.

Someone has said trusting Jesus Christ as Savior means marrying adventure, living by faith, and expecting the unexpected. Do your friends and family see you experiencing pleasure, fulfillment and adventure in faithfully serving the Lord on a daily basis? What is involved in fulfilling your God-given responsibility throughout your journey of life?

Dare Enough to Go

Jesus gives two primary directives to people: COME and GO. He first asks us to COME to him for salvation and to continue coming to Him for wisdom, strength, comfort and rest.

"Jesus stood and cried out, saying, 'If anyone is thirsty, let him come to me and drink. He who believes in Me, as the Scripture said, from his innermost being will flow rivers of living water.'"
(John 7:37-38)

"Come to Me, all who are weary and heavy-laden, for I am gentle and humble in heart, and you will find rest for your souls."
(Matthew 11:28)

Many Christians never take seriously Jesus' second directive-GO. They are content to come to Jesus for salvation and comfort yet ignore his command to GO. The New Testament is filled with commands for believers to go into the marketplace and influence others for good. Jesus spoke personally of the need for people to go and share what God has done in their lives. Some of the last words spoken by Jesus concerned the subject of "going."

Mickie, a long time friend, was twenty-two when her mother lost the battle with cancer. Recently Mickie said, "Over the years, I have often wished my mother had written me a letter before her death, telling me she loved me, giving encouragement and anything she wanted me to know. It would have been such a treasure." If you knew you had only a few days to live, what would you share with your loved ones? You would undoubtedly say the things most important to you. When Jesus was nearing the end of His time on earth, He gave some important, parting words to his disciples.

"Go therefore and make disciples of all the nations, baptizing them in the name of the Father and the Son and the Holy Spirit,

teaching them to observe all that I commanded you; and lo, I am with you always, even to the end of the age." (Matthew 28:19)

The last words of Jesus were meant for our ears and hearts as well as those of the disciples. Most Christians realize the command to GO applies to them but choose to disobey the directive. God has the right to expect His children to obey His commands and disciplines us for disobedience.

When my husband and I married, we bought a used refrigerator and kept it for several years. It was long before the days of frost-free technology and the small freezer compartment regularly became encrusted with frost. One day I realized it was well past the time for defrosting the freezer. Although my children had lived with the refrigerator all their lives, I suddenly felt the duty to warn them of a danger. I turned to my five-year-old daughter and eight-year-old son and said, "Kids, whatever you do, don't ever touch this freezer with wet hands, your tongue or anything like that."

Upon issuing the warning, I went outside to mow the lawn. Before I could start the mower, the back door flung open, out ran my daughter, and she began to scream, "Come quick!" I asked, "What's wrong?" She threw her head back, stuck her tongue out and said, "Jeff said, 'GO GET MAMA.'" I did not quite understand so I asked again, "He said WHAT?" She stuck her tongue out as far as it would go, "Jeff said, 'GO GET MAMA!'" Suddenly, I realized what happened and ran into the house. Sure enough, there was Jeff, hanging to the freezer by his tongue.

Quite irritated I said, "The last thing I told you NOT to do was stick your tongue to the freezer. Did you hear me say that?" He muttered (as best he could with his tongue stuck to the freezer wall), "Uh huh." "THEN WHY DID YOU DO IT?" I yelled. "I don't know," he mumbled. I began to melt the frost with hot water and started the parental lecture. When his tongue was almost free, he jerked back, leaving a chunk of tongue on the freezer. Yuck! Of course I left it there for days, enabling him to see how disobeying his mother brings pain!

Jeff was clearly disobedient to the last words I said to him and he suffered the consequences. Likewise, the majority of Christians are disobedient to the last words of Jesus, "GO." The consequences of disobedience can be painful. *Lost blessings are always a consequence of the failure to follow Christ's commands.*

- Have you become so comfortable in your religious retreat you ignore His heartfelt words "Go into all the world?"
- Would you go <u>anywhere</u> the Holy Spirit led you?
- Where might He want you to go?

Dare to Go Across the Pew

Religious people often pride themselves in showing others how "righteous" they are when they are only self-righteous. Some attend church as they would a social club and others delight in the honor of leadership within the church. These misguided motives are actually a show of religious power and bring untold strife in the body of Christ. However, Paul urged the Ephesian Christians to strive for unity, not power.

"I, therefore, the prisoner of the Lord, entreat you to walk in a manner worthy of the calling with which you have been called with all humility and gentleness, with patience, showing forbearance to one another in love, being diligent to preserve the unity of the Spirit in the bond of peace." (Ephesians 4:1-3)

The rupture in the fellowship of the body of Christ is rampant in America and this must break the heart of God. Self-righteous people are wounding the One who suffered for them by insisting on getting their way. *Selfish service results in a flawed fellowship and a tainted testimony.* This leaves the church open for an attack from the world.

I heard that when a group of thoroughbred horses face attack, they stand in a circle facing each other and with their back legs kick the enemy. Donkeys do the opposite; they form a circle, face the enemy and kick each other. How often do church members mimic donkeys? They ignore the real enemy while attacking fellow believers.

Do you have a "donkey" in your church or is there someone you do not particularly like? There may be valid reasons for your dislike of this person, yet God calls us to be peacemakers. God may ask you to go across the pew and initiate a renewed fellowship with that individual.

Some years ago, Sally (name changed) moved from the north to Murfreesboro, Tennessee, due to her husband's employment. She hated the South, she hated the way we talked, she hated the weather and she hated her husband for bringing her to such an unenlightened area.

She joined my church and was faithful in attendance. However, at every opportunity, she verbalized her disdain for all things southern. Her greatest delight was in mocking the drawl of anyone who dared to speak in her presence. This was not an attempt at humor but the epitome of harshness. She crossed the line when she corrected the wording of a new Christian who had bravely said his first public prayer. Needless to say, she won no quick friends. Soon my disdain for her was greater than her disdain for the south!

After listening to a Spirit-filled sermon one Sunday, I told God I would go anywhere He wanted me to go. I envisioned going to some god-forsaken place like Somalia but instead He told me to go to Sally! He spoke quietly in my spirit, "Go tell Sally you love her." "OH NO," I thought, "I would rather go to Somalia!"

I began to argue with Almighty God, "Lord, You know I don't like Sally and Your Word says you hate hypocrites. I would be a big hypocrite if I told Sally I love her so I really shouldn't do it." God spoke again, "Go tell her you love her." My reply, "But I don't love her!" God chided me, "You better love her; I love her."

I knew the stirring in my spirit was from God but I simply did not want to obey. At the same time, I felt reasonably sure Sally was already gone. She always sat on the back row and was the first to leave since she had no friends. However, I turned around and saw Sally standing alone by the door.

Several people made decisions that particular Sunday and since I was a Sunday school teacher, I felt it my duty to shake hands with everyone and invite them to my class. Of course, my real motive was to give Sally plenty of time to get out of the church!

Finishing my handshaking duties, I glanced to the back again and there was Sally; she had not moved a muscle. I determined God had frozen her in place so she could not leave until I quit arguing with Him. I began my trek toward Sally, speaking to everyone along the way, silently hoping she would manage to leave.

As I walked slowly to where Sally was standing, God spoke to me again, "HUG Sally and tell her you love her." My mind was flooded with regret that I had not obeyed immediately. God had upped the ante and now I had to HUG her! What would all my friends think; what would SHE think? A southerner probably had never hugged her and I had a feeling she did not want to start now. I straightened my back, furrowed my brow and headed for the guillotine.

Walking up to Sally, I hugged her and said, "Sally, I want you to know I love you." She gave me a questioning look and said sarcastically, "Well, thank you." I added, "I know you are new to this area and if you ever need anything, I will be glad to help, like recommending a doctor, grocery store or restaurant." She stared at me with beady eyes then asked in an unpleasant tone, "Would you come to my house for coffee tomorrow morning?" My mind was shouting, "NO," but my mouth said, "I would be glad to come." I spent the remainder of the day fretting about the visit. I was concerned she would attack someone dear to me and my disdain for her would pour out on her kitchen table.

The next morning in great fear and trepidation, I drove to her house. She greeted me at the door and we began small talk. Within five minutes, she started to cry and tell me her life's story. She was abused from the age of four, married at a young age to escape her home life, and had two children by the age of eighteen. Her husband was killed in an accident at the age of nineteen; she remarried only to find her second husband was physically abusive. She had two more children and felt completely trapped.

Sitting at Sally's kitchen table, I was convicted by the Holy Spirit. If I had lived the life of Sally, I probably would not be on the back row of any church; instead, I would be at home in a heap of self-pity. Understanding the extreme difficulties of her life gave a new perspective on her behavior. Instead of my disdain flowing out on the table, my tears of empathy mingled with hers and a friendship was born.

I wish I could say Sally became a sweet person due to our relationship but that would not be true. However, God mellowed her harsh words and we remained friends until she moved away. God knows the heart and He knew Sally needed His touch of love, given through another person. However, my judgmental spirit almost prevented His working.

- Would you be willing to go across the pew to a person you dislike for the sake of unity?
- Would you welcome anyone to your church, regardless of race, lifestyle, or financial status?
- Would you be willing to befriend someone who is down and out?
- Would you search your heart to determine if you have a judgmental spirit?

Religious people often have judgmental spirits and become a detriment to the Lord's work. They refuse to go in love to someone who has failed or spiritually fallen. They possess a holier-than-thou attitude, which hinders lost people from finding Christ and discourages struggling Christians.

A New York family bought a ranch out West where they intended to raise cattle. Friends visited and asked if the ranch had a name. "Well," said the would-be cattleman, "I wanted to name it the Bar-J. My wife favored Suzy-Q, one son liked the Flying-W and the other wanted the Lazy-Y. So we're calling it the Bar-J-Suzy-Q-Flying-W-Lazy-Y." The friends asked, "But where are all your cattle?" He sadly replied, "None survived the branding."

Unfortunately, many people do not survive the judgmental branding of some Christians and this mindset affects the unity of the church. To follow the example of Christ, our attitudes and actions must change. Christ ate with publicans and tax collectors; he associated with sinners; he touched lepers. *Christ never had a judgmental attitude although he was the Perfect Judge.* He extended His love to all and asks nothing less of His children.

Has your pew become a religious retreat of inaction or are you willing to bring unity to the Body of Christ? Until we are at peace with our brothers and sisters in Christ, we are ill prepared to be God's servants in the world. Daring to go across the pew is preparation for the next destination.

Dare to Go Across the Street

God is systematic in His plans and He places us in certain locations to live, work and play. *He is sovereign in His placement and single-minded in His purpose.* Intending for His children to reflect Christ in these locations, He intertwines our lives with those who need a Savior and Comforter. Occasionally, the placement is not pleasant and we cannot see a loving Hand in the action. However, God sees far into the future and we are blessed if we can see clearly the events of today.

Corrie ten Boom and her sister, Betsie, suffered a living hell in the Ravensbruck concentration camp during a war that took the life of everyone in their family. Before Betsie died, she described God's sovereignty in a way that changed Corrie's life. Betsie weakly whispered, "I don't know why God allows suffering, Corrie; all I know is across the blueprint of our lives, God wrote the word *Ravensbruck.* Tell them, Corrie-tell them that no pit is so deep that God's love is not deeper still. They will listen to you because you have been here."

We do not get to choose the exact blueprint of our lives. *We have the choice to accept God's design rather than demand a change.* Anyone looking at Betsie and Corrie's situation would wonder how a compassionate God could allow His children to suffer in such a place. However, Corrie rested in God's plan and said, "The higher the view we have of His sovereignty-that our times are in His hands-the greater will be the possibility to live in victory." Corrie ten Boom's testimony of faith inspired millions as she traveled the world telling of God's love. Do you want to live in victory? It is found in becoming useful to God, regardless of the location He has chosen for you.

God has orchestrated a network of lost and hurting people within our realm of influence, many of whom we see daily. They are neighbors, store clerks and co-workers; He has allowed our paths to cross theirs for a purpose. If we are spiritually open to divine appointments in our community, God will use us in dramatic ways.

My husband and I completed a long day of working on our lawn and were returning a borrowed truck. We were tired, hungry and in a hurry to get home. Driving down a dark country road, we saw a red Volkswagen parked on the shoulder. The sight was not unusual, as many patrons of liquor stores in the neighboring "wet" county would lose their ability to drive as they returned to their "dry" county homes. Noticing a woman in the driver's seat, I mentioned she might be having car trouble. My husband replied, "Oh you know she hasn't had car trouble, she's drunk." We drove past the car a few hundred feet and God nagged at my heart. I decided to put Danny on a guilt trip by asking, "If I had car trouble, wouldn't you want someone to stop and help?" Guilt worked; he turned around and went back.

He parked the truck behind her car and walked to the driver's side window. Knocking on the window, he asked if she needed help. At first he thought she was asleep because her head was resting on the steering wheel, which confirmed his suspicion she was drunk. He started to walk away when she looked up and mouthed, "I need help." Opening the door, he saw the reason for her inability to drive. There was a blood-covered towel in her lap; she had slit both wrists in an attempt to commit suicide. He motioned for me to help and we attempted to stop the flow of blood. She was going in and out of consciousness and something had to be done immediately.

Due to the distance from an ambulance service, we knew the only hope of saving her life was to drive to the hospital. I sat in the passenger seat; Danny picked her up and put her in my arms. On the way to the hospital, she occasionally cried and muttered a few words; they always concerned her four young sons. She kept saying she did not want to die and leave them alone. I mentioned I was a Christian and was praying for her. I also gave her the only hope I could give, Jesus Christ. She said she wanted to believe in Jesus and then lost consciousness.

Although the woman had lost a vast amount of blood, she was still alive when we arrived at the hospital. The emergency personnel assessed her condition, started blood transfusions and told us they thought she would survive. After admitting her to the hospital, we left but I returned the next day to inquire about her status. I learned she was in critical condition but had been asking about the couple that brought her to the hospital. She was not allowed visitors but the nurses thought it would be a calming influence if she could meet the person who saved her life.

I was apprehensive but entered the room to find an attractive, young woman who was grateful to be alive. She said, "After I slashed my wrists, I kept thinking about my four little boys. I did not want to die. I didn't know anything about prayer but started begging God to make someone stop and help me. Cars passed and the blood would not stop; I knew I was going to die alone in the car. I gave up all hope but then you stopped. I want you to know I heard what you said about Jesus and I trusted him as my Savior." She was crying but this time she was crying tears of joy. We kept in touch for years and she continued to grow spiritually and raise her boys to know the Lord.

God had a purpose for our being on the lonely stretch of road that night. We were only interested in getting home and resting our bodies; God was interested in saving a life and giving eternal rest. His is a much higher purpose. We never know at the beginning of a day, what divine appointments await us before the day is done.

- Will you ask God to give you divine appointments of ministry?
- Will you take a risk by stopping to help someone in need?
- Will you watch for opportunities rather than look the other way?
- Will you dare to go across the street to share Jesus with your neighbor?

"Go out into the highways and along the hedges, and compel them to come in, that my house may be filled." (Luke 14:23)

Dare to Go Across the World

Ann often says God's will is geographic; our responsibility is to determine where in the world He would have us serve. The scope of our vision is small compared to His. We are preoccupied with our work, families and church; He is concerned about a world filled with people who have no hope. God gives a calling to every Christian to go wherever He directs them. However, our view of God's calling to "go into all the world" is colored by prejudice, fear, lack of resources, and a perceived inability to be useful. What a different world it would be if Christians adopted God's view, His strength and His purpose.

"For God has not given us a spirit of timidity, but of power and love and discipline. Therefore do not be ashamed of the testimony of our Lord, or of me His prisoner; but join with me in suffering for the gospel according to the power of God, who has saved us, and called us with a holy calling, not according to our works, but according to His own purpose and the grace which was granted us in Christ Jesus from all eternity." (II Timothy 1:7-9)

Personally going. Most of us are hesitant to make a commitment to go abroad in service to the Lord, especially with the tension in the world today. War, terrorism and other dangers deter us from fulfilling our responsibility. We convince ourselves the need is greater "here than there" when we have not conversed with the Maker and Master of the world. He makes it clear the only hope for mankind is for Christians to be willing to go and share His love where there is a drought of His Word. *We may be timid in our commitment but God is not timid in His command.* He tells us go wherever the Spirit sends us.

In the summer of 1998, I received a letter from a large missionary-sending agency asking me to pray about participating in a mission trip. Having been on several foreign mission teams, I was not completely surprised until the letter stated the destination, the Islamic Republic of Iran. I walked into my kitchen, put the letter on the table and said aloud, "I don't think so; a person would have to be stupid to go into Iran. I am NOT going." Subject closed! I began working around the house and God spoke in my Spirit, "You are telling Me, Almighty God, you are NOT going to do something?" I called Ann to tell her about the letter and she had gotten the same invitation. I told her, "I do NOT want to go." She wisely replied, "I don't either, but we have to pray about it." I did not want to pray because, somehow, I knew if I did, God would have me on my way to Iran.

During the next few weeks, Ann and I felt a definite call from God to make the trip to Iran in spite of the danger. We began saving our money and emailing the missionary with whom we were to work. On August 7, 1998, television newscasts were filled with reports of simultaneous bombings of United States embassies in Kenya and Tanzania and the terrorists were traced to Iran and Afghanistan. The agency sponsoring the trip cancelled it. Ann and I heaved a huge sigh of relief. We thought, "God just wanted our willingness." However, we received an email from the missionary asking us to complete our commitment. The decision was made more difficult when we learned the team's responsibilities included smuggling Bibles and tracts into Iran. We began to pray fervently to determine God's will. We found God's will did not change with the bombing of the embassies or the cancellation of the trip by the denominational agency. Preparations began to recruit one hundred prayer warriors in our home churches to pray for our safety during the trip.

The Sunday before we left for Iran, my pastor asked the church to pray for me and the three other ladies on the team. He stated for security reasons, we could not tell the name of the country where we were going. He stressed the fact this was a dangerous area of the world and prayed for God's protection. I deeply appreciated the prayers of my church and their concern.

Following the end of the service, I wondered if my seven-year-old granddaughter, Olivia, was upset by the mention of danger. I called my son and he said Olivia cried all the way home from church. Later in the afternoon, I took Olivia to get ice cream. On the way, I tried to explain how a Christian must be obedient to God's leading. She said, "La La, I do not want you to go. Bro. Dean said it was a dangerous place and I am afraid for you to go." She started crying again and I continued to reassure her that this was what God asked me to do.

Attempting to change the subject, I said, "Olivia, you know I usually bring you a little church from the country in which I am working; I can't bring you a church from this place." She asked, "Why not? You always bring me a church." I explained there were no churches in this country because they did not know about Jesus. She straightened up, wiped away her tears, put her hands on her hips and said, "Well then, La La, you have to go!" The words tumbled out of a pure seven-year-old heart; if people did not know Jesus, then someone had to go tell them. I was reminded of the scripture that says, **"A little child will lead them,"** and I was proud of her evangelistic fervor.

Ann and I smuggled Bibles into Iran, left tracts everywhere we went, prayer-walked, shared our Christian testimony and lived to tell about it. We often wonder why God was adamant about our going on this mission trip and eternity will reveal the results of our efforts. Christians are not responsible for the results but are called be a part of His redemptive work.

- Would you go <u>anywhere</u> God asks you, depending on Him for everything?
- If God has not asked you to travel across the world, is your responsibility any less than others who serve in far away places?
- What can you do to enable the Good News to be spread?
- Are you willing to sacrifice your comfort for Christ?

If God has not called you to travel to a distant land and endure the rigors of foreign living, you may be experiencing a feeling of relief. Strange food, extreme weather conditions and indiscernible language make international missions a difficult assignment. God does not release you from the command to GO even if you never set foot on foreign soil. The world desperately waits for your answer to God's call.

Faithfully giving. A. T. Pierson said, "There is enough jewelry, gold and silver plate buried in Christian homes to build a fleet of 50,000 vessels, ballast them with Bibles, crowd them with missionaries and supply every living soul with the gospel in a score of years. Only let God take possession and the gospel will wing its way like the beams of the morning." Americans spend seven times more money on pet food each year than they do for all charitable giving. *It cannot be pleasing to God when we care more for our pets than we do for people.*

Your call to GO may involve sacrificially giving of your resources yet most of us know nothing of true sacrifice. We give from our excess, after we have spent the majority of resources on ourselves. God delights in the sacrificial gift for His Kingdom's work. Jesus watched as a poor widow came into the temple and placed two small, copper coins in the temple treasury. He made a stunning statement to his disciples.

"Truly I say to you, this poor widow put in more than all the contributors to the treasury; for they all put in out of their surplus, but she, out of her poverty, put all she owned, all she had to live on."
(Mark 12:43-44)

This widow blessed the heart of Jesus and He blessed her in return. Her sacrificial gift is still an inspiration to all who read the account. Likewise, a wonderful Christian woman in Murfreesboro, who is a widow also, has inspired many. We affectionately call her Miss Eula. She is now ninety-two and continues to faithfully serve the Lord. Although Miss Eula always has a smile on her face and encouraging words on her lips, she has experienced many sorrows. Her husband died at an early age and one year later, her twenty-six-year-old daughter died in a tragic automobile accident. The daughter, Nancy, was weeks away from graduating nursing school and was engaged to be married. Miss Eula speaks often of her daughter and the close relationship they shared.

As I was preparing for a mission trip to Chile, Miss Eula asked if I had any particular needs. I told her the team was collecting used eyeglasses, which would be given to the extremely poor people in Chile. She made no comment but approached me a week later with something in her hand. She said, "I have kept Nancy's glasses prominently displayed in my living room since the day she died over 30 years ago. It is the only thing I have left of hers. God began to speak to my heart about sending Nancy's glasses to someone in Chile." She continued telling about her struggle in releasing the glasses; I told her I understood and she needed to keep them. "Oh, no," she said, "God told me to give them away and I must be obedient." As gently as you would handle a new born baby, she laid the glasses in my hand and enclosed them with my fingers. In sacrificial love for the Lord, she had given the last tangible vestige of her daughter. She smiled and said, "It would be selfish of me to keep Nancy's glasses when someone needs them. Take them with my love."

I collected over a hundred glasses and packed them in a box for the flight. However, Nancy's glasses traveled in my purse like a treasure. Upon arrival in Chile, we began giving away glasses and ministering to the people. We placed boxes of glasses on a table and the Chilean people would attempt to find a pair that enabled them to see. I told the missionary the story about Nancy and she immediately called my attention to a young woman who was frantically searching through the boxes. It seemed none of the glasses corrected her vision and she had a look of disappointment on her face. She was approximately the age Nancy was at her death and I wondered if this was to be the recipient of Miss Eula's heartfelt gift. I reached into my purse and handed her, ever so gently, Nancy's glasses. She put them on and began to exclaim, "I can see, I can see, I can see." Joy spread throughout the room and I think there was joy in heaven.

Unlike Miss Eula, most of us cling to our possessions and selfishly deny the opportunity for lost people to see Jesus. Sacrificial giving involves anything that is important to us.

- Would you be willing to give your last cent so another would know Christ?
- Would you be willing to sell all you have and give to it the poor?
- Would you be willing to give your treasured things for eternal rewards?

"Do not lay up for yourselves treasures upon earth, where moth and rust destroy, and where thieves break in and steal. But lay up for yourselves treasures in heaven, where neither moth nor rust destroys, and where thieves do not break in or steal; for where your treasure is, there will your heart be also." (Matthew 6:18-19)

Fervently praying. It is our God-given responsibility to passionately pray for those around us who do not know the Lord or are in need of His touch. Ann and I meet every morning to pray for our children, grandchildren and others with personal needs. We had the special blessing this fall of learning about the salvation of my son-in-law's daughter, Lauren. She came into my family at the age of seven and although I do not get to see her often due to distance, she has been a blessing to us. She is now a beautiful eighteen-year-old young woman ready to graduate high school. For eleven years, Ann and I prayed for Lauren. We rejoiced with Wade and Jenise at the wonderful news, witnessed her baptism, and praised God for answered prayers. Many people prayed for Lauren's salvation and it was a personal blessing to see the fruit of our prayers. Ann and I continue to pray daily for Lauren and look forward to seeing how God is going to use her in His service. We should never underestimate the power of our prayers.

Andrew Murray said at the World Missionary Conference in 1910, when asked what was needed on the mission field, "We shall need three times more men, four times more money, and seven times more prayer." *Every Christian is called to travel across the world on their knees.* Ann often states in our Iran presentation, "Our prayers can take us where our feet will never go." Prayer always precedes power and power is needed to change the world for Christ. Therefore, we have the responsibility to see the ministry and mission through the eyes of faithful, fervent prayer.

If God's people were committed to labor in prayer, Christ would reign in many more hearts and the world situation would be changed drastically. God is waiting for His people to pray; will you dare go into the world by way of God's throne room?

"The effective prayer of a righteous man can accomplish much." (James 5:16b)

Care So They Will Know

"Seeing the multitudes, He felt compassion for them, because they were distressed and downcast like sheep without a shepherd." (Matthew 9:37-38)

Jesus saw the needs of the people who were in His realm of influence and His heart was broken. He was filled with the compassion of the Heavenly Father and took steps to alleviate the pain of the hurting. However, people in religious retreat have a closed mind, a hardened heart and hands that are slow to aid the helpless. Ministry is spiritually useless unless we have the Lord's compassion as a basis for all we do.

Open minds. If we are to escape the religious retreat and walk in divine adventure, we must possess an open mind to God's leadership and those to whom we minister. This does not happen automatically or easily. Our closed mindset can be damaging to our Christian witness. Our opinions are influenced by many factors, including parental training, life experiences and society's standards.

Jesus was not hindered by a closed mind; He was not offended when a known sinner approached him at dinner and wiped His feet with her tears and hair. Others were offended by her actions but Jesus defended her against the accusers. An open mind does not mean approval of the sin but rather an acceptance of the sinner.

"Now one of the Pharisees was requesting Him to dine with him. And He entered the Pharisee's house and reclined at the table. And behold, there was a woman in the city who was a sinner, and when she learned that He was reclining at the table in the Pharisee's house, she brought an alabaster vial of perfume and standing behind Him at His feet, weeping, she began to wet His feet with her tears, and kept

wiping them with the hair of her head, and kissing His feet, and anointing them with perfume." (Luke 7:36-38)

To overcome the years of negative input, it is necessary to change our mental attitudes. We must allow God to cleanse our minds of the things that shut people out of our lives. As we seek to have a mindset of ministry, regardless of the need, God will revamp our way of thinking.

The first step in "caring so they will know" is to think the thoughts of Jesus Christ. If we think loving thoughts about another person, it will greatly determine our emotions and actions.

"For as he thinks within himself, so he is." (Proverbs 23:7)

Tender hearts. Scripture tells us to "walk in love" and this means pouring freely our compassion on those who desperately need it. As we minister to hurting people, we should leave them better than when we came. When people feel like a project instead of a person, they are further demoralized and defeated.

Ann and I have a mutual friend who is a leader in a mission organization. She was not raised in a Christian home; in fact, no one in her family was a Christian. As a child, she was painfully poor. Her father disappeared, leaving her mother with four young children and it was difficult for her mother to earn enough money for the basic needs of the family. There was a large church in her town and occasionally some women came to their door and brought used clothing in a garbage bag for the children. She said they would grab the bag, pour out the contents and everyone would be filled with great excitement.

However, after she grew older, she began to notice how the women looked at her mother. It was a look that said, "You could do better if you really tried." She knew how hard her mother worked to put a roof over their heads and food on the table. The women would stand in the doorway and hand the bags to her mother and it was obvious they did not want to touch her.

Our friend shared, "I decided as a young girl I would never become a Christian because of the way those women looked at my mother. After several more years of their "ministry," I hated Christians and I hated the church due to the attitudes I witnessed. However, one day a woman came from the same church with another garbage bag of clothes. She stood in the doorway and talked with my mother like a good friend. She asked if she could visit awhile, came in and sat on the couch. I don't know why, but I climbed into her lap and she put her arms around me as she and my mother talked. I was hot, dirty and much too old to be so forward but something was different about her. The woman returned for another visit and began to share what the Lord meant in her life. The love of Jesus was reflected in her love for my mother. Mother accepted the Lord as her Savior; eventually all four children were saved." This story had a happy ending, not because someone ministered, but because someone ministered in love.

- Are you willing to be vulnerable with your emotions?
- Could you love a poor person as easily as the well-dressed visitor at church?
- Will you allow the love of Jesus to be evident in your ministry?

Willing hands. It is good to have an open mind and a tender heart but God commands us to put those characteristics into action. To be dedicated followers of Christ, we need to get our hands dirty. Ministry is seldom clean, sanitary or pleasant; yet, it brings great joy and fulfillment.

Ann shared earlier about the ministry of our mission team to Babe in the Appalachian Mountains. Words cannot describe the sights and smells of her house but our love for Babe was not determined by the circumstances. A lady on the team, Linda Moore, was working at a cool, clean ministry point. She prepared materials before she came and was enjoying teaching the children. However, God began to work in her spirit and by mid week, she asked if she could clean Babe's house. She did not make this decision out of ignorance because she heard every day how terrible the situation was in which to work. That did not deter her from climbing on the van the next day with a smile on her face. She literally scraped cat hair from the walls, scrubbed everything from ceiling to the floor, mopped, cleaned windows, and used a ton of cleaning supplies. She endured the smells, cat manure and fleas; she never lost the smile on her face. Though such ministry left her bone-tired, it gave her a sense of joy in knowing her hands had been symbolic of God's willing hands. May it be so in your life!

It is our God-given responsibility to dare to go where He leads us and to care for those with whom we minister. Physical and emotional ministry is important and Jesus' life demonstrated those qualities. The goal of all ministries should be the glory of God. Jesus called attention to His Father often and He is our example of ministry and witnessing.

Share from the Overflow

It is incredibly easy to talk about something that is important to us and we do it all the time. If a man is a "sports nut" you do not have to beg him to tell you the latest exploits of his favorite team, especially if they are winning. If a woman is an accomplished shopper and has found the world's best bargain, she will tell about it repeatedly.

Over the years, I have questioned why grandparents talk so freely, boldly and consistently about their grandchildren. Given half a chance, they tell everything about their little darlings.

- First steps-even if they were bribed with candy.
- Funny sayings-even if they were embarrassing.
- Potty training-even if it was at the age of six.
- School activities-even if they had to make up something.
- Grades-even if the only A was in P.E.
- Sports-even if they were benchwarmers.
- Good looks-even if you know they are relatively ugly.

I simply did not understand the bragging of grandparents. I did not have any grandchildren and none was on the horizon. My son, Jeff, and his wife, Deborah, had been married for five years and she had not been able to get pregnant. They were both Christians and I prayed God would bless them as He saw fit. When my children married, I made a commitment to pray for them and their mates every day. One day as I was praying for Jeff and Deborah, my eyes fell upon a scripture that almost jumped from the page:

"And as for Me, this is My covenant with them," says the Lord: "My Spirit which is upon you, and My words which I have put in your mouth, shall not depart from your mouth, nor from the mouth of your offspring, nor from the mouth of your offspring's offspring," says the Lord, "from now and forever." (Isaiah 59:21)

When I read the part about "your offspring's offspring," I knew in my heart this was a promised child for Jeff and Deborah. Later that day, Jeff came to the house and God impressed on my spirit to share the scripture. I resisted because I was afraid I had not heard correctly. Yet, God kept nudging me and eventually I said, "Jeff, you and Deborah are going to have a baby." He gave me a, "you are crazy," look and grunted. He obviously thought his mother had lost her mind. I explained further, "God told me this morning through scripture you are going to have a baby." He gave me another look that said, "You are crazier than I thought." Regardless of the looks, I dated the scripture in my Bible, March 16, 1990.

A few months later, Deborah told Jeff, "If I did not know better, I would think I was pregnant." Stunned, Jeff said, "Well, I know Mom has been praying." She went to the doctor and it was confirmed she was indeed pregnant. Her due date was March 16, 1991, exactly one year after the date God had spoken so clearly. However, she was told there was a high likelihood of a miscarriage due to some physical problems. Sure enough, she went into premature labor at four months.

Jeff called me from the hospital and said Deborah was being admitted. My husband and I hurried to the hospital, praying fervently. Upon arrival, the only thing I could tell them was, "God said you are going to have a baby; I don't know if it is this baby but you are going to have a baby!" They were able to stop the labor but in the sixth month, she was put to bed for the remainder of her pregnancy.

On February 26, 1991, Olivia Claire Outland came into this world, a bit premature but healthy and beautiful. I cannot explain the joy I felt when Jeff came into the waiting room with the little bundle in his arms. Here was my "little boy" holding his child and my first grandchild. The joy was made even sweeter because of the long wait and the fulfillment of God's promise. I took a hundred pictures and showed them to everyone I saw including the hospital janitors and cafeteria workers. No one escaped my unrestrained joy. I understood fully from that day forth why grandparents talk freely, boldly, and consistently about their grandchildren. It is because we love them so deeply.

- How does this unrestrained joy compare to the joy you have in the Lord?
- Is it as easy to talk about Jesus as it is your children, grandchildren, hobby or anything else that is important to you?
- Do you share freely your testimony?
- Are you bold in your witness?
- How consistent are you in sharing your faith with non-believers?

If the answers to the above questions leave you feeling somewhat guilty, then you are like the majority of Christians. Most Christians have difficulty sharing their faith. Why? Could it be our love for the Lord has grown cold because we have been in a religious retreat? How can we maintain an overflowing joy and witness?

Persistent Prayer

John Bunyan said, "He who runs from God in the morning will scarcely find Him the rest of the day." We must cultivate an intimate relationship with God by spending time with Him. Do we get as excited talking with our Savior as we do talking with a friend? Unfortunately, many Christians pray in times of crisis but have no intention of making a commitment to persistent prayer. Most people say they believe in prayer but know little about true, heartfelt prayer.

Two men were talking and the first challenged the other, "If you are so religious, let's hear you quote the Lord's Prayer. I bet you ten dollars you can't." The second responded, "Now I lay me down to sleep, I pray the Lord my soul to keep. And if I die before I wake, I pray the Lord my soul to take." The first pulled out his wallet and fished out a ten dollar bill, muttering, "I didn't think you could do it!" We may laugh at this illustration, yet fail to follow Christ's teaching on prayer and an intimate relationship with the Father.

If we love our family, we want to be around them and communicate our love. The same is true with God; He wants us excited about being in His presence, communicating, and drawing close to Him. **"Draw near to God and He will draw near to you." (James 4:8)** The closer we are to God, the more joy fills our hearts.

Consistent Bible Study

Nothing takes the place of consistent, personal Bible study. God has left us a love letter and it is an affront to His love when we neglect to read His words. Is daily Bible Study important to you? Sometimes our quiet time with the Lord becomes a time to read other things. *If we are not careful, we profusely read good books but not the Good Book.* Amy Carmichael once said, "Never let good books take the place of the Bible. Drink from the well, not from the streams that flow from the well."

It is said that when David Livingstone started his trek across Africa he had seventy-three books in three packs, weighing 180 pounds. After the party had gone three hundred miles, Livingstone chose to throw away some of the books because of the fatigue of those carrying his baggage. As he continued his journey, his library grew less and less, until he had only one book left, his Bible.

We cannot have an overflowing testimony if we do not fill our minds and hearts with the Word of God. Would you commit to make consistent Bible Study the most important item on your schedule?

Walking Like Jesus

It is not difficult to share from the overflow when we have spent time with Jesus in prayer and Bible study. When we nurture a relationship with God, walking in obedience is a natural occurrence. Our lives take on new meaning and we are transformed people. How would your life change if you walked in obedience to the promptings of the Holy Spirit?

Before her death of ovarian cancer, Gildna Radnor, a comedienne on Saturday Night Live, told of an event in her childhood. Gildna's family had a little dog that was like a family member, very loved and appreciated. The little dog was close to delivering puppies and they were watching her closely. However, one day Gildna's mother was mowing the lawn when the little dog ran in front of the mower, cutting off her back legs.

The mother and children were crying hysterically but they wrapped the dog in a towel and took her to the veterinarian. After examination, he told the waiting family the dog could be saved and he thought she could have the puppies with no problem. However, he thought it best to put her to sleep since she would have a difficult time getting around with only two front legs. The family could not make the decision to put her to sleep so she had surgery and they brought her home.

It took only a week for the little dog to get around the yard. She would take two steps with her front legs, stretch as far as she could and flop her backside over. She would get up, and repeat the motions. She learned how to get around quite well. In two weeks, she gave birth to four puppies. She nurtured, fed, and loved them. When the puppies learned to walk, they walked just like her, taking two steps with their front legs, stretching as far as they could and flopping their backsides over! The sight was strange but they lived so close to their mother, they walked just like her!

God wants us to live so close to Him we walk, talk and live just like Jesus. *Our walk may look strange to sinners but satisfying to our Savior.* Will you dare to go, care so they will know and share from the overflow? Spiritual growth begins in the church pew; spiritual maturity moves us outside the church walls to the masses. Ministering and witnessing are no longer chores but **"Christ in you, the hope of glory." (Colossians 1:27b)**

Chapter 5

Victorious Vessels

"But in all these things we overwhelmingly conquer through Him who loved us." Romans 8:37

Section 1

God Talk

As normal American kids, my children desired and acquired a variety of pets in their growing-up years. We gave away as many as we adopted because Mom refused to take on the responsibility for the animals Rad and Michelle "thought" they wanted. Two guinea pigs passed away in our care, and I insisted Michelle return a dog given by her boyfriend as a Christmas present during high school. Overall, we were not a pet family; nevertheless, I have one dog story that trumps most animal brag sessions I have heard.

The children found an abandoned dog during an outing at the local airport with their dad. She was promptly named Kibbles and brought home in the back of the pickup truck. A puppy at the time, she remained an "outside" dog except in extreme weather. We had a kennel area in the side yard with water, doghouse and fence. My husband installed a metal wire from the kennel fence to a tree, tied a roller wheel and rope to Kibbles' leash, and she was able to run in the yard the length of the rope. The children were assigned the responsibility of feeding the dog; the parents took her to the vet for shots and sick visits. Kibbles thrived in spite of the fact the children paid her little attention after the first month.

I had a neighbor who truly was a "pet person." Mr. Gilley was a retired engineer, bachelor, and uncle to some of my good friends. His dog, Billy Joe, had been acquired from the pound and was a mixed breed, but Mr. Gilley wrapped his life and affections around his dog. You would have thought he paid a million dollars for him. Billy Joe went everywhere Mr. Gilley went, sitting on the front seat of the pick-up every time it left the driveway. As a new single mother, I sensed Mr. Gilley was not impressed with my pet care abilities compared to his, but I learned how far off the mark I was when he rang my doorbell one day.

"I know you are having a hard time handling the house, the yard, and the dog by yourself. Would you like me to take Kibbles to my house and care for her?" he asked. I was stunned by his offer, but readily agreed I was having a hard time transporting Kibbles to the vet. Kibbles went next door to live that day, and we saw her in the back of Mr. Gilley's truck and

Billy Joe in the front seat almost every time he left. The children would occasionally walk over and pet her, but Kibbles quickly adapted to the royal treatment she received from Mr. Gilley and adjusted to her new home.

Several years later, I moved to another city. Both children were in college and Kibbles was forgotten. I had entrusted her to someone who obviously loved her more than we did, with the time and resources to care for her. A couple of years later, I learned Mr. Gilley had passed away, and his niece had become the trustee of his estate. Both dogs went to live with her, and Kibbles was completely lost to our family. I happened to run into the niece at a funeral one day, and she brought up the subject. "Did you know Billy Joe passed away shortly after my uncle died?" "No," I responded, "I guess he grieved himself to death. What about Kibbles?" "Oh, she's fine, living with us," she said. "Did you know my uncle left $50,000 in his will for the care of the dogs?" Shocked would not begin to describe my demeanor. "You mean Kibbles is now worth $50,000?" "Yes," she answered. "Well, if you decide you cannot keep her, let me know," was my weak response. "Oh, I think we can handle her," she winked.

Our unwanted pet, Kibbles, the dog abandoned at the airport, given to a neighbor, had more money than I did! I was amazed at her good fortune. This little dog, who had nothing to offer the world other than a warm nose, was now an heiress! I realized it does not matter *who* you are; it matters *whose* you are. The relationship to Mr. Gilley made all the difference in her life. The same truth applies to the Christian life. We are part of an extraordinary lifestyle when we enter into relationship with Jesus Christ, no matter how ordinary we are. We become heirs to His kingdom and He has untold blessings to share with us, His children. It is all about *relationship*!

"I pray that the eyes of your heart may be enlightened, so that you will know what is the hope of His calling, what are the riches of the glory of His inheritance in the saints, and what is the surpassing greatness of His power toward us who believe." (Ephesians 1:18-19a)

God desires us to know Him intimately and live the victorious life He fashioned us to enjoy. Spiritual intimacy is nurtured in the same way other relationships grow-through daily communication and time investment. Just as Kibbles loved Mr. Gilley because he cared for her, we gravitate toward the people who genuinely care for us. Jesus Christ wants to be as real to you as your closest family member. His love for you is without parallel in human experience. In fact, the model God provides us in the scripture for His desired relationship is the Bridegroom as He relates to His Bride, the church. There is no more intimate relationship in life than the complete intimacy found in marriage, yet God loves us even more than a spouse. He desires to commune, nurture, guide, protect, and bless His people daily. The way to enjoying Him is to invite His presence and develop a spiritual sensitivity to His voice.

Talking with God

The key element to an intimate relationship is open communication. Christians refer to conversation with God as prayer, but people of beliefs systems other than Christianity engage in the same exercise. During our trip to Iran in 1998, Carolyn and I saw people fall to their knees on prayer mats five times daily, beginning before dawn. They prayed fervently to Allah as a pillar of their religion. The uniqueness for Christians as they pray is the confirmation that prayer draws them to God and moves Him to action. Prayer is not a ritual to advance a person's position before God, but rather communion with a living Lord. It is the natural communication that characterizes a vital relationship. Prayer requires action, love, and effort as well as verbal exchange.

I remember the first Christmas my son-in-law, Jay, spent with our family. At our Christmas Eve gift exchange, I asked each family member to share something for which he was grateful. Because he had only been dating my daughter a short period of time, Jay expressed gratitude that he had been included at our gathering. "My desire is to be back here, sitting in this room, next Christmas." And he was, but not because of a simple desire. Jay courted, pursued, and convinced Michelle to marry him during the following year. The next Christmas, Jay was not only a part of the family Christmas gathering, he was engaged to marry my daughter.

I see in Jay's experience a parallel to prayer life. Simply stating a desire to spend more time with the Lord is not enough. A rote recitation of memorized prayers at meal and bed times is not enough. We must pursue a love relationship with the Savior. Our hearts should long for companionship, communication, and deeper commitment to the One who loves us. Thoughts of time spent with the Savior should flood our memory as we joyfully anticipate each minute in His presence. A grateful Christian will set aside special moments of prayer, but he will also communicate quietly and persistently throughout the day.

"Pray without ceasing." (1 Thessalonians 5:17)
"Devote yourselves to prayer, keeping alert in it with an attitude of thanksgiving;" (Colossians 4:2)

Constant prayer seems an unobtainable goal, yet the scripture admonishes us to do it. Effective prayer is like a telephone call in which no one hangs up the receiver. It is an open, never-ending conversation with God, continuing throughout the day and into the night. We share our thoughts, fears, questions, and opinions without inhibition as we go through our day. If we had a loved one in the intensive care unit of the hospital, we would not have a problem praying fervently and constantly. Our world is sick, critically ill, and God urges His people to pray without ceasing.

Hundreds of books have been written on the subject of prayer, and I find myself facing a daunting task to add anything more to explain its wonders. Several years ago, Carolyn and I had a denominational training session in Arizona, so we took an extra day and drove to Grand Canyon National Park. I was apprehensive about the day, not knowing what to expect or how long to plan our stay. Carolyn was beaming with confidence as she pulled her camera out of the backseat. "Oh, don't worry. It won't take long. I'll put my wide-angle lens on the camera, take a few shots, and we'll be on our way." Three hours later we were still riding a tour bus around one rim of the canyon and had not begun to capture all the wonder of this remarkable place. So it is with prayer. There is no way to explain its beauty and depth in words. It would take a lifetime to explore the magnitude of God's desire to relate to His children, yet I will share some thoughts from my years of experiencing God through prayer.

The Inward Journey of Prayer – Praying for Myself

Before we can pray for others, there are several ways in which we need to pray for ourselves. Most have no problem praying selfish prayers for health, happiness, success, and material gain. We also find it easy to spend volumes of time praying for our children and grandchildren. There are deep, spiritual requests God would have us make of Him. These prayers answered will lead His children to treasure chests of spiritual blessings God desires for His followers. In fact, some of these inward requests must be made before we can expect answers to outward prayers.

Forgiveness. Growing up in the 1950's, I experienced the privilege of having a stay-at-home mom. My mother spent her days cleaning, shopping, cooking, and taking care of three children and a husband who worked long hours. Her goal when my father returned from work was for everything to be spotlessly clean, including herself. She worked tirelessly all morning in older clothes, sporting a variety of aprons. Around two o'clock in the afternoon, however, her appearance began to change. She bathed, rolled her hair, and applied make-up. We had only one car, so she finished dressing and combed her hair by five thirty, and piled all of us into the old Chevrolet to pick up my dad from work at the hardware store. When my father entered the car, his bride was sparkling clean and sweet smelling.

In the same manner we need to enter God's presence as a pure, spotless bride, free from the dirt and grime of sin. The book of Ruth is a beautiful story of a bride being purchased by her kinsman/redeemer, Boaz, a type of Christ. The night Ruth approached Boaz to request her redemption, she is advised by Naomi to alter her appearance.

"Wash yourself therefore, and anoint yourself and put on your best clothes, and go down to the threshing floor; but do not make yourself known to the man until he has finished eating and drinking." (Ruth 3:3)

In like manner, David, after his sin with Bathsheba was exposed, approaches God by asking for cleansing.

"Be gracious to me, O God, according to Your loving kindness; according to the greatness of Your compassion blot out my transgression. Wash me thoroughly from my iniquity and cleanse me from my sin. Create in me a clean heart, O God, and renew a steadfast spirit within me." (Psalm 51:1-2, 10)

The dirt of daily sin can taint us and requires a habitual request for forgiveness as we enter God's presence. People who would not dare skip their daily shower may go for weeks or months without asking for conviction and cleansing from sin. While we may not be engaging in what we term "big" sins, the more insidious, subtle sins of life can coat our white garments, turning them dingy brown. Carolyn once used a dramatic visual in a conference where she poured clear, fresh water out of a clean pitcher into a crystal glass. She asked the conferees how many would be willing to drink water from the glass. Everyone agreed they would not mind drinking the water. She then poured a tablespoon of dirt into the pitcher, poured another glass, and asked again who would be willing to drink it. No one wanted the water. Even what we term a "small" sin brings us into God's presence sullied, dirty, and unacceptable to His sinless nature.

When Jesus died upon the cross and shed His blood, He made the perfect sacrifice for our sin. He took upon Himself the punishment for our transgressions. Our *position* before God is perfect due to Christ's sacrifice. However, as we enter His presence, we must seek cleansing from the sin of daily life marring our *fellowship* with Him.

"**If we say we have no sin, we are deceiving ourselves and the truth is not in us. If we confess our sins, He is faithful and righteous to forgive us our sins and to cleanse us from all unrighteousness.**"
(I John 1:8-9)

Years ago, as I was teaching a ladies' Sunday school class, the door opened and a young woman slipped into the rear of the classroom. She sat in rapt attention, hanging on every word. As the class concluded, she raced to my desk and said, "I want what you were talking about." "What do you mean," I asked incredulously. "I want a relationship with Jesus." It stunned me and I grabbed the class president as she headed toward the door, asking her to stay. We sat with this young woman on the first row of the class and she began to pour out her life's story. She confessed one sin after another in a steady, therapeutic stream. There was no coaxing on our part. When the Holy Spirit convicts of sin, there is a desire to confess and be cleansed. We were able to pray with the young lady and claim God's forgiveness in light of her admission.

I have met people who begged God repeatedly to forgive them of sins they perceived as too ugly to be covered by God's grace. You may be struggling with such a sin in your life. Let me caution you; forget your feelings and claim the facts! God has promised to forgive us if we confess our sin, repent of it (turn around and head the other direction), and claim His power to cover our sin with His grace.

My daughter made a profession of faith at a young age. Although she had grown up in church and received wonderful training in our children's department, I wanted the pastor to speak with her before she joined the church for baptism. He explained sin as being covered with mud and the need to shower daily from its grime. His word pictures were graphic, tailored for a child. A few days later I was mowing the back yard, and Michelle and her little brother were playing in the front yard under my watchful eye. I noticed Michelle was going back and forth to an outside water faucet at the front of the house, carrying water in a small bucket to the rock garden. I was happy the children were playing peacefully and did not question the activity. When I finished mowing the yard, I went to gather them for baths and supper. To my amazement and chagrin, I discovered Michelle had been mixing mud in the rock garden and had literally covered Rad with it from head to toe. All I could see of my precious son were two blue eyes, peering out of a brown face. They were both so mud-caked I had to hose them off before we could enter the house. I told my pastor the next week he might need to tone down his sin story!

You may feel like one of my children, totally encrusted with sin, not just slightly dirty. The burden of past indiscretions may weigh heavily on your mind and in your spirit. Remember the *pristine* experience I related in chapter one? If God says you are pure and forgiven, then claim your new life and begin living in freedom. The world may label you. You may have applied a faulty label. If you have confessed and repented, God's opinion is the only one that matters. You are what He says you are–forgiven and clean.

Insight. God desires for us to see the world as He sees it. Although we will never be like Him, God seeks to give us divine insight as we view the circumstances and people around us. Only then can we relate to people and problems in a Christ-like manner. Godly insight into problems is called wisdom. Godly insight into the nature of people is called discernment. Wisdom and discernment are worthy requests as we approach the Father in prayer. Wisdom enables us to find God's will for decisions in life; discernment allows us to feel God's heart toward people. It is God's will for all people to be brought to a saving knowledge of His Son, Jesus. It is God's heart for people to be drawn by His love and compassion.

"For God so loved the world that He gave His only begotten Son, that whosoever believes in Him shall not perish, but have eternal life. For God did not send the Son into the world to judge the world, but that the world might be saved through Him."(John 3:16-17)

I have often said when God wants to change the world,

- He does not send an earthquake.
- He does not send a tsunami.
- He does not send a war.
- He sends a baby.

Jesus Christ came as a baby–God incarnate, born in the poorest of places, the lowliest of circumstances, yet He saved the world. Babies, the tiniest and most helpless of all creatures, have the power to turn hearts as nothing else.

My friends Katia and Hector recently had their second child. Both parents are in their early forties and have a fourteen-year-old son. Katia had experienced two miscarriages and had given up trying to have another child when she discovered she was pregnant. The pregnancy was normal and the family was assured the baby was healthy. She entered the local hospital for a routine delivery, but things went terribly wrong. As the contractions became more frequent, Katia suddenly began to hemorrhage and was rushed to surgery. Baby Nathanael was delivered by C-section but not until he had been deprived of oxygen for nine minutes. Katia was airlifted to a Nashville hospital while Nathanael was taken to a different hospital by ambulance.

Katia's family was told she had little chance of survival and the baby would be severely brain damaged.

After seven days and numerous blood transfusions, Katia was released from the hospital, but Nathanael's prognosis was much worse. After thirty-three days, he was sent home under hospice care. This committed Christian family, emigrants from Cuba, was devastated. As I attempted to comfort Katia one day, she commented, "I don't know what the Lord is trying to teach me. I already know compassion. We have had numerous families live with us; I have cared for sick people in my home for weeks at a time. I know compassion. What is He trying to teach me?" I answered quietly, "Maybe He is trying to teach other people the need for compassion."

Nathanael, a tiny baby who cannot cry, who will never see, hear, or talk, fed through a tube from nose to stomach, has already impacted more lives than he could have ever touched healthy. Our Sunday school class generously donated money to help the family with medical bills and living costs. Numerous people, some strangers to the family, have visited the home to pray for Nathanael. A lady arrived one day, walked to the door with an envelope, and said she could not stay. The envelope contained $1,000. Little Nathanael has changed not only his family, but also everyone who has allowed his situation to touch the heart.

Will you allow God to teach you compassion from His insight of the world? Today I found myself unsatisfied with the size of my condo, wishing for more square footage to entertain family and friends. I tuned into a program on television reporting poverty in America. Forty-two percent of single mothers and their children live below the poverty line. Most of the homeless in this country are single mothers with small children. I wept as I realized how God blessed me during my days of single parenting and asked Him to forgive me for wanting a larger house. I am so blessed to have a home.

Anderson Cooper of CNN, reporting on the problem of homelessness, said the people who are able to overcome their situation are those with determination and at least one person willing to help. Many times the one person is a social worker. Would it not be wonderful if the one person were a Christian church member, one with a heart filled with the compassion of God? Why should we care? We should care because God cares. We need to pray for His heart and His vision of the world. Praying for insight will give us a new heart because we will see the world as God sees it, hurting and needy. Our desire for more will be turned into a desire for *others* to have more.

Influence. I pray for God's heart of compassion but I also pray for Christ's heart to know and do the Father's will. Because it is the Father's will to bring eternal salvation to men, I want to participate in His plan. He asks us to use our lives to influence others to become all God desires them to be. President Eisenhower was once asked the key to his success as a general and president. He revealed his discovery "the important things are rarely urgent, and the urgent things are rarely important." The Father would have Christians to make the important thing, the urgent thing. He asks us to look for ways to share Him with people, no matter how small or insignificant the opportunity appears.

Several years ago, my maintenance man at the apartments shared his twenty-eight-year-old son was dying with cancer. He refused to take chemotherapy because of a drug addiction and the cancer was winning. Peter (name changed) had three young children, no job, no income, and was spending his last days at his mother's home under hospice care. I regularly gave his dad money to help with expenses; when Peter died, his dad, uncle, grandfather, and I paid for his burial. I had prayed for months for Peter's health and salvation; as I looked into the coffin, I immediately noticed a fabric cross lying across his denim shirt. "Was Peter a Christian?" I asked. "Yes, he became a Christian when he was in grammar school. He was saved at Vacation Bible School," replied his dad. "What is the story behind the cross?" I inquired. "Oh, he made the cross at VBS the summer he was saved. His mother always kept it," he responded.

I thought of how rowdy this young man might have been that summer at VBS. I wondered if his teachers knew the impact their efforts had on this young man and his mother. I thought about the children I have been privileged to influence through friendships, school teaching, and children's programs at church. Had I influenced them for the Kingdom? How many people have I influenced to become better? All of us have an effect on those around us. Only we can determine if our influence is for good or evil, for temporal things or for eternity.

Peter was a Christian who strayed far from the Lord in his short life, but God used his childhood salvation to draw him back to spiritual values before death. The hospice minister who preached his funeral shared Peter rededicated his life and asked to be baptized again in his mother's bathtub. Peter died at peace and in the presence of his Father because of the efforts of several Vacation Bible School leaders and others willing to influence him during his last days.

Influence extends to other Christians, as well as those outside the Kingdom. What am I doing to influence younger or less mature Christians to a life of ministry and service? Most of what we desire to share is caught rather than taught from a servant lifestyle. In 1982, I was required to attend a leadership conference for missions' volunteers in our association of churches. The meeting was fifty miles away, the weather was cold and rainy, and I was still breastfeeding my son. Barely concealing my foul mood at having to leave my family for the evening, I climbed into a van to travel with eight other women to the meeting. As we entered the church, the associational leader accompanied me to the door of a conference she said I needed to attend. Determined to "endure" the meeting, I glanced at my watch, and began to fidget.

The conference leader, an older woman, began the meeting by announcing she would not be teaching a book, rather she wanted to motivate us to carry out the principles of ministry. She began to relate example after example of personal witnessing and ministry from her life. I was totally mesmerized; here was a Christian doing what Christ instructed His people to do. She was actually living a life of ministry and verbal witness daily. At thirty years of age, I had not met anyone so dedicated to unselfishly give herself to people in need. Jo Waldrup immediately became my model for ministry.

I ran into Jo at another state meeting a few months later and shared with her how much the conference had touched my heart. She immediately said, "Well, thank you, but what have you done with it?" I felt as if she had taken a basketball and shoved it into my stomach. I had to admit to her and myself that I had done nothing with the newfound insights. I made the commitment to enter a lifestyle of ministry, and I have no regrets.

Jo Waldrup's influence extended far beyond 1982. In 2006, Carolyn brought me a clipping from a Nashville newspaper highlighting Jo, now age eighty-nine, as she entered the women's prison to lead Bible studies and worship for the inmates. Her service is a lifestyle; her influence lives on, not only through her present efforts, but also through me. Everyone I touch is her fruit as well. Thus, the legacy of influence continues far beyond one person. Let our prayers be for positive influence to affect both those inside and outside God's Kingdom.

The Intercessory Journey of Prayer – Praying for Lost People

God gifts His children with the ability to pray for others, both at home and around the world, through intercessory prayer. I read a quotation, which impacted me significantly. "We have no right to talk to lost people about God until we have talked to God about lost people." Prayer is the prerequisite for witnessing. Intercessory prayer is a precious gift, and God wants us to ask Him *how* to pray for others. No one can bring another person into the Kingdom; only God through the power of the Holy Spirit can convert a soul. However, God desires to use our prayers to influence others for the Kingdom. Intercessory prayer is powerful and effective, but years may pass before we see the results of our efforts. Prayer can be likened to a seed, placed in the soil of faith, and growing requires time.

As a child in Southeast Alabama, I was blessed to have extended family living in close proximity. My mother's parents lived two blocks from us on the same street, and my brother Jim was a frequent guest at their home. In fact, he spent nearly every afternoon at his grandparents with unlimited access to their television. My grandmother petted Jim and spent a lot of time playing with him. One afternoon she announced they were going to learn how to grow potted plants. She took Jim to her back stoop where they placed dirt into a clay pot, planted several seeds, and watered them. The next afternoon, my six-year-old brother returned to their home, grabbed his snack, and proceeded to the television set. My grandmother, however, announced they needed to go outside and check the potted plant.

Jim was quite young but extremely intelligent. He replied he did not believe the plants had time to grow, but Grandmother insisted he go outside with her. There on the stoop was the pot with a cluster of lollipops in it! "You didn't know we planted lollipop seeds yesterday, did you?" My brother was enchanted and thoroughly enjoyed the lollipops. Imagine his disappointment when the suckers were gone and he learned the terrible truth. THERE IS NOT SUCH THING AS A LOLLIPOP SEED! Prayer is not a lollipop seed that sprouts beautiful, sweet results over night. It requires nurture, waiting, and possibly years to yield God's results. *Intercessory prayer is for the committed, not the impatient.* There are several ways God would have us pray for unbelievers.

Pray for God to draw people to Himself.

"No one can come to Me unless the Father who sent Me draws him; and I will raise him up on the last day." (John 6:44)

Our desire for others should be their entrance into a personal relationship with God through His Son, Jesus Christ. As we enjoy the ability to enter God's throne room through prayer, our thoughts should be for others to do the same. However, the reality is God must do the drawing; we only assist Him by befriending and sharing His love with non-believers.

In the 1980's, I had the privilege of attending Castle Hills First Baptist Church, my brother's home church at the time. Castle Hills is a suburb of San Antonio, Texas, and Jim was stationed at Ft. Sam Houston. As I entered the sanctuary of the church, I was overwhelmed by the presence of the Spirit; I cried through the song service and most of the sermon. When we returned to Jim's house, I asked him and his wife, Becky, "What is different about your church?" He told me in the 1970's, when Jack Taylor was pastor, he and the deacons felt led of the Lord to walk around the perimeter of the property weekly. They prayed for lost people to be drawn to the church campus. People began pulling off the expressway, entering the church and saying, "I don't know why I'm here. I felt so drawn to stop." Someone on the staff would ask, "Are you a Christian?" Eventually, someone had to be on duty at the church all the time because many people were walking into the facility, inquiring about spiritual matters. Castle Hills First Baptist grew tremendously during this time as more and more people were saved. The amazing aspect of the story is that the Spirit is still drawing people to this church, thirty years later. I shared the story in a conference near Memphis recently. An Asian lady approached me during the break, crying. She told me two of her adult children are members of Castle Hills First Baptist, and she has the same spiritual reaction each time she enters the church.

We need to ask, "Would I be willing to give myself in prayer for lost people to be drawn to my church?" Consider organizing a prayer-walking group in your church to pray for the property and the surrounding neighborhood. God may be waiting for your willingness to pray so He can work. I do not understand why the Lord of the universe waits upon His people to pray, but He does.

Carolyn and I are blessed to be members of Belle Aire Baptist Church in Murfreesboro, Tennessee. In the past seventeen years, the average attendance has grown from approximately two hundred and fifty to fifteen hundred under the leadership of our pastor, Dr. Dean Sisk. We never lose sight of the fact it is the Spirit who does the drawing. Many people who enter the doors of our church later say, "I felt God's presence as soon as I entered the sanctuary." Is God's Spirit a welcomed guest at your church? Only He can draw people into the Kingdom, and He waits upon our prayers to move.

Pray for Truth to be revealed to unbelievers.

"Thomas said to Him, 'Lord, we do not know where You are going, how do we know the way?' Jesus said to him, 'I am the way, and the truth, and the life, no one comes to the Father but through Me." (John 14:5-6)

We live in a world of conflicting philosophies and belief systems. Many expound the view it does not matter what you believe as long as you are sincere. The Bible contradicts this concept. Jesus boldly announced in John 14:6, there is absolute truth, and it is found through following Him. Henry Blackaby says, "Truth is a person, Jesus Christ." People outside the Kingdom cannot understand spiritual matters unless God reveals truth to them. Otherwise, they are content to be nurtured by the values of a world system ruled by Satan.

An emergency room doctor related the story of a young woman he examined who was weak and lethargic. Because her symptoms were general, a series of diagnostic tests were ordered. The routine chest X-ray revealed her esophagus was glowing, as if she had swallowed barium. The doctor questioned the young woman and asked her if she had swallowed or eaten anything unusual. She refused to answer the question. At the same time, her blood work revealed extreme anemia. The doctor sent the support personnel from the room and again questioned the woman. She finally admitted she had been eating dirt.

The doctor explained to me when a person becomes extremely iron deficient, her body senses there are minerals in the dirt and she will ingest it, seeking relief. Of course, the body does not process dirt, and it passes through, offering no help or nutrition. In the same way, empty habits and philosophies look appealing and promise to meet needs but offer no nurture or encouragement to seekers. We are surrounded by a society offering the dirt of alcohol, drugs, pornography, and illicit sex. Those choosing to satisfy valid needs with inadequate resources are left deficient, needy, and heart sick. There is an alternative.

"Jesus said to them, 'I am the bread of life; he who comes to me will not hunger, and he who believes in Me will never thirst.'"
(John 6:35)

Hunger and thirst, emotionally and spiritually, are the result of our need for God. Jesus Christ is the only way to have our needs validly and eternally met. The eyes of lost people are blinded unless God lifts the veil and allows them to see.

"And even if our gospel is veiled, it is veiled to those who are perishing, in whose case the god of this world has blinded the minds of the unbelieving so that they might not see the light of the gospel of the glory of Christ, who is the image of God."
(II Corinthians 4:3-4)

Our witness to the world needs to be the Truth of God found in His Son, Jesus Christ. I boldly proclaim He is the only way to heaven. We must affirm the true Gospel as we deal with people in love. *Truth and love can be dispensed simultaneously.*

Pray God will send someone to witness of His presence and power to save.
When we pray for God to send someone, we must realize "someone" may be me! Many people are frightened at the prospect of sharing Christ, fearing they will offend or not know what to say. We have made witnessing far too difficult both in our minds and through our approach. Witnessing is simply sharing Christ in everyday conversations, what He means personally and what His presence has accomplished in our lives.

The easiest way to encourage people to listen to the Gospel is to invite them to your church. When new Christians are interviewed, the most common reason they have for attending a church is that someone invited them, not an ad in the paper or a sign on the road. In 1995, my pastor asked me, with the help of three young couples, to begin a new coed Sunday school class. Avery and Gina, neighbors to the host couple, attended our first fellowship meeting. Gina had recently been converted. She had been invited by her brother to a revival service at a church in a neighboring city. During the invitation she was drawn by the Spirit to make a profession of faith. However, Gina and Avery were not attending church in our city; hearing about the new class, they quickly joined.

Within a few months, Avery made a profession of faith and both were baptized. Avery and Gina invited his sister to attend our class; and within a few months, she and her husband made professions of faith and were baptized. When I left the city to move to Murfreesboro, Avery's brother-in-law had invited his sister and her husband to our Sunday school class and church services. No one "trained" these young couples in witnessing. They simply invited those they loved to find the Living Water they were enjoying. Within the first year I taught the class, there were eight professions of faith from our ranks, simply because people invited their loved ones to church.

We need to assure newcomers are welcomed into our local churches once we invite them. Carolyn and I frequently speak at women's events in churches across our convention. Often, we are amazed how few people approach us with a greeting or with conversation. We wonder if strangers entering the church will receive a warm reception. A greeter system with people at the entrances to welcome guests and direct them to classes and the worship center is a wonderful way to relieve the anxiety of visitors. As we pray for people to witness, we need to pray for nurturing churches to disciple the new converts.

God networks the lives of unbelievers with Christians to be a lighthouse of Godly influence. In answer to our prayers, God will send someone to witness to our lost loved one if we are faithful to witness to those around us. Years ago, my grandfather was dying, and I was terrified he was not Christian. He lived over eight hundred miles away and was too sick for me to have long conversations with him on the phone. I prayed desperately for him and enlisted many of my friends to pray. I was distraught when he died, not knowing his eternal destination. When I arrived at the graveside, the assistant pastor of my parent's church preached the service and shared how my grandfather came to saving faith before he died. I had been faithful to pray, and God had been faithful to send a witness.

Talking About God

We naturally talk about the people and things we love. I have two children whom I treasure; as the reader has moved through this book, you have learned about Rad and Michelle. In the same manner, people will know the depth of our love and commitment to God by listening to our conversation and watching our lifestyle. If a stranger entered your home, would there be evidence of your Christian faith? Do your coworkers and acquaintances know of your commitment to the Lord after talking with you? There should be no undercover Christians! It is valid to ask ourselves some questions about verbal witnessing.

- How much scripture should I memorize?
- Should I take a witnessing training course?
- How do I know when to say something for Jesus?
- Why am I afraid to witness?

While this book is not designed to be a witnessing training manual, I will seek to address some of these concerns.

Say what the Spirit leads you to say.
Scripture memorization is wonderful, and I encourage everyone to memorize as much of the Bible as possible. Witnessing training is helpful, and I would advise all Christians to take training when it is available. But the most important aspect of verbal witnessing is to follow the leadership of the Spirit in our remarks. Not every comment we make is designed to lead someone to the Lord. We may be planting seeds with the nuggets of spiritual truth we use in normal conversation and actions. A young lady from our congregation spent almost three years as a missionary in Southeast Asia. During her training, Emily was presented with this question: If every conversion were to take ten spiritual conversations, sowing seeds of Christ, would you be willing to always be person number nine? As we talk to an

unbeliever, we may be the first Christian to present spiritual ideas and philosophies; we may be the third or fourth. If we are obedient to speak as the Spirit leads, we can trust God to use other people and situations to draw the unbeliever to Him.

Several years ago, I was in need of medical insurance and was contacted by an independent insurance agency. A husband and wife team came to my door at the appointed time and went through their sales pitch. I decided to buy the coverage, wrote a check for the first month's premium, and voided a check to be used for bank draft information. As I handed them the checks, my mouth opened and words I had not planned spilled out. "Thirty minutes ago, you were complete strangers to me. I have given you money and access to my commercial checking account. And they say it takes a lot of faith to trust in Jesus Christ."

The husband immediately dropped his pen with a thud on the tabletop and looked at his wife. I was sure I had offended them until he said, "I have been talking to her for months about how to have a relationship with Jesus." I knew instantly the Spirit had prompted my comment. For half an hour the husband and I discussed with his wife about having a personal, faith relationship with the Lord. She had religion and relationship confused and had allowed hypocritical Christian leaders to disillusion her. I was sure God used our conversation as one of the "seeds" to grow her faith. Although I did not see her come to saving faith during our visit, I was obedient to say what the Spirit impressed on my heart. I am equally sure God sent others into this woman's life to witness of His saving power. I am content to sow seeds rather than reap a harvest every time.

The secret to any spiritual comment is the power God places behind it, not our ability to speak a polished presentation. Tony Campolo, nationally recognized evangelist, author, and professor, tells a story perfectly illustrating the point. As a boy, he attended a church camp with a group of friends. At the camp was a boy afflicted with cerebral palsy. He jerked and stuttered, and the other campers mocked him unmercifully. Around the campfire the last night, leaders asked the boys to testify of their growth in faith during the week's experience. Thinking they were too cool to say anything, the boys sat in silence. Finally, the spastic boy haltingly stood up to speak. Tony and the others snickered, elbowed each other, and rejoiced at another opportunity to ridicule the young man.

Stammering he said, "I..I..I..I love J....J...J...Jesus, and J...J...J...Jesus l...l...l...loves m...m...me." After these halting words, before anyone else spoke, the Spirit of God descended on the group. Men and boys began to weep and pray. Tony Campolo related it was the night God called him to the ministry. Tony did not know at the time, but years later learned, several other young men had been called the same night to full-time ministry through the Spirit-filled words of a handicapped boy. Just say what the Spirit leads you to say. His power will use your words for His purpose.

> "But God has chosen the foolish things of the world to shame the wise, and God has chosen the weak things of the world to shame the things which are strong, and the base things of the world and the despised God has chosen…" (I Corinthians 1:27-28a)

Be what the Spirit asks you to be.

Actions speak louder than words. We have grown up hearing and using this adage, but its truth is amplified in the spiritual. It is the presence of God through His Holy Spirit, which empowers our testimony and brings spiritual victory. Have you noticed how much is learned about a person by studying her demeanor? There are some individuals whose smile and warmth literally invite closeness, admiration and love. I see Jesus in some of my truly spiritual friends. They are approachable and inviting. I believe Jesus was such a person, and He asks us to be mindful of our "being" as well as our "doing."

Nell Bruce, a legendary prayer warrior and pastor's wife, led a prayer retreat for our association many years ago. She told a story I will never forget, which I believe sums up the core of personal witnessing. After many years of ministry and marriage, Nell's husband was admitted to a nursing home. He was in a coma; although his condition usually ravaged the features of its victims, his face remained serene and peaceful. From the time of his admission, her husband was not able to utter a word or pass a conscious look. His primary care nurse was not a Christian, and Nell attempted to witness to her at every opportunity, to no avail.

Late one night, Nell received a phone call; her husband was in his last minutes. She hurried to the nursing home, but he had already passed away by the time she arrived. The primary care nurse was there and told her, "It was time for my shift to end, but I knew Mr. Bruce was critical. You were not here, so I decided to stay with him until he passed. In his last moments, I was standing at the foot of the bed; his face and then his whole body began to glow. Mrs. Bruce, I want you to know I was overwhelmed by the presence of God. I stood next to the bed, held onto his leg, and I gave my life to Jesus."

Nell's husband had not said a word to his nurse. The power and presence of God's Spirit had convinced this woman to make a life-changing decision. Nell had been faithful to talk. God had been faithful to draw. I am reminded of the words of Elizabeth Elliot. "I can think of no clearer analogy of our place in God's service and no more accurate picture of the relative merits of who we are and what we have to offer. We shall always be just pots, but what we carry for others is priceless."

"Lord...we are the clay, and You our Potter." (Isaiah 64:8)

In the power of God, simply *be* what He made you to be. He will do the work. He will win the victory through His vessels, as we allow Him to mold, remold, and use us.

Section 2

Our Walk

It was a steamy, hot night in July when a visiting evangelist in our small, country church captivated my attention. Despite the lack of air-conditioning, I was excited about another night of revival services. At the age of five, my excitement was not due to deep spiritual insight but by the fire and brimstone preaching of the speaker. His picturesque description of hell was vivid and riveting.

Our pastor was somewhat boring, speaking in monotone; the evangelist was a wonderful change of pace, yelling and rattling the windows with his voice. His sentences ran together until he was breathless; he gasped and began again. Running back and forth across the front of the church, he waved his arms and stomped his feet. He wore a black suit with a red tie and began to sweat profusely after a few minutes of preaching. Unable to endure the coat because of the heat and physical activity, he dramatically removed it and threw it on a pulpit chair. I was mesmerized by his vocal and animated delivery of the sermon. I normally went to sleep immediately after the song service but it was impossible to nap through this man's gut-wrenching sermons about hell and its consequences.

After a few nights of listening to the intriguing speaker, I decided to become a "preacher" with the same characteristics. As my daddy worked in the fields and my mother cooked dinner, I began the transformation from a timid, little girl to a dynamic evangelist. From my daddy's closet, I retrieved a black suit coat and red tie; I grabbed his big, black Bible and headed outside. A preacher needed a congregation so I began to search for the best place to begin my evangelistic career.

Gazing around the back yard, I spied approximately one hundred chickens enclosed within a fence. They became my captive audience as I climbed onto a chicken coop and began my tirade. With a shrill, five-year old voice, I screamed to the top of my lungs all the words the evangelist had spoken the previous night. Beginning to sweat, I threw daddy's coat unto a nearby stump, all the while letting my red tie swing back and forth in the wind.

Chickens are easily excitable and my shrieking voice upset them; they began to squawk and run around the fence. At first the chicken's reactions were an encouragement, comparable to "amen" from the congregation. However, the louder I screeched, the louder they squawked and the more distracted they became. It seemed the only recourse to getting their attention was to turn up my tone a decimal, which only made matters worse.

From the field, my daddy heard a commotion at the chicken house. Determining a fox was killing the chickens, he ran to chase the culprit away. Coming through the clearing in the woods, he saw a sight not to be forgotten. He said, "I saw a little girl wearing a big red tie, holding a huge Bible and standing on a chicken coop. Unable to get the chickens to listen she yelled, 'Well chickens, just keep squawking, go to hell, and see if I care.'"

Unfortunately, most Christians have this mentality about unbelievers who surround them. It has been reported 96% of Christians never share their faith with anyone. We may be faithful in church attendance and lead relatively "clean" lives. Yet, we silently tell our neighbors, coworkers and friends, "Just go on working, playing, living and go to hell for all I care." These words would never come out of our mouths. However, if we fail to share the good news of Jesus Christ, our lives give the message clearly that we do not care about their eternal destiny. Are you going through life's journey with the seeds of the gospel still in your possession? Will you determine to sow as you go in order that others will be brought into the Kingdom? Nothing compares to the joy of having a part in a soul coming to know the Lord; it is the extraordinary life at its best!

"He who goes to and fro weeping, carrying his bag of seed, shall indeed come again with a shout of joy, bringing his sheaves with him." (Psalm 126:6)

When life comes to an end, may none of us meet Christ with empty hands but instead bring with us many who have come to faith through our life and witness. How can we become victorious vessels and walk in a way that draws people to Jesus Christ?

Walk a Guided Path

Christians can be comforted by the knowledge we are not alone in this world. The Holy Spirit is given to us as a guide for every decision and step we make. God wants His children to have clear direction for their lives and places the Spirit within us for that purpose. God's wisdom is ours for the asking if we appropriate the power of the Holy Spirit within us.

"But when He, the Spirit of truth, comes, He will guide you into all the truth; for He will not speak on His own initiative, but whatever He hears, He will speak, and He will disclose to you what is to come." (John 16:13)

"Things which eye has not seen and ear has not heard, and which have not entered the heart of man, all that God has prepared for those who love Him. For to us God revealed them through the Spirit; for the Spirit searches all things, even the depths of God." (I Corinthians 2:9-10)

Stepping into the Darkness

Before God can use us to the fullest, He calls for some changes in our lives. It is easy to be deceived concerning our true motives for service. God wants to shine His piercing light into the dark areas of our hearts through the Holy Spirit. If we are honest, we do not like what we see. Therefore, we often quench the working of the Spirit in our lives lest we see the darkness in our hearts. Following the search light of the Holy Spirit, what revelations would we discover if we stepped into the darkness of our hearts?

The Holy Spirit reveals my selfishness. It is amazing how selfish we can be with our time, spiritual gifts and resources. Our culture has convinced us our *wants* are primary over the *needs* of others. We set our own agenda concerning the use of God's provisions. All the while, we profess Jesus to be Lord of our lives. We simply do not want the Holy Spirit to have total control over our life. Why?

- Schedules would change.
- No long-term plans.

- Circle of friends would be more inclusive.
- Money would not be our own.
- Priorities would change.
- Hearts would be burdened for the lost.

Do you look at this list and fear God will radically change your life if His Spirit completely guides you? Without a doubt, He will turn your life upside down and inside out; a life consumed with a devotion to God cannot remain the same. Selfishness is a barrier to living as victorious vessels; it is preventing us from being filled with the Spirit, following His directions and living the abundant life. Do you want the Holy Spirit to fill you to overflowing? Ask God to reveal the selfishness in your life.

The Holy Spirit reveals hidden sin. Pride prevents us from acknowledging our sin; therefore, we are handicapped in our spiritual walk. Christians are masters at masking their marred hearts. Although we look spiritually healthy to the casual observer, our hidden sin is open to the all-seeing eye of God.

"The heart is more deceitful than all else and is desperately sick; who can understand it? I, the Lord, search the heart, I test the mind, even to give to each man according to his ways, according to the results of his deeds." (Jeremiah 17:9-10)

We are afraid to admit our weaknesses, even to ourselves; hidden sin eats at the very fabric of our spiritual life. God would have us delve into our hearts and allow His light to guide us to repentance. Will you allow the Holy Spirit to reveal and clean your heart of hidden sin?

In the fall of 1970, my husband's employment required our family to move to Memphis, Tennessee. I have never been a spotless housekeeper and became even more lackadaisical since I knew no one would be visiting my home. The first week was filled with hanging pictures, placing furniture and organizing closets. When Sunday arrived, I was ready for a "day of rest." After visiting a nearby church, I prepared for my family a delectable lunch of frozen pizza. Immediately after eating, I left the plates, glasses and pizza crust on the table and retired to the recliner. I proceeded to read the thick, Sunday newspaper and after finishing each section, I threw it in the floor.

At 2:00, the phone rang and a lady identified herself as Mrs. Gill, my Sunday school teacher that morning. We had a casual conversation and then she asked, "Could my daughter, Sandra, and I visit you sometime?" I politely said, "We would love to have you visit." She quickly responded,

"We are free to come now, would that be all right with you?" I looked around the house and nothing about a visit seemed all right to me! The children had thrown their coats and shoes on the couch, there was a pile of newspapers by the recliner, and Danny was carving a Jack-o-lantern in the middle of the den floor. To make matters worse, I had piled the dirty breakfast dishes in the sink because I did not have a dishwasher, not to mention the lunch mess still on the table.

Horrified at the thought of having her come to my house, I stood with the phone in my hand. The silence was embarrassing and suddenly I heard myself say, "Why sure, come on over." Hanging up the phone, I began barking orders, "Kids, get the coats, shoes and newspapers, throw them on Jeff's bed and shut the door; surely they won't ask to see the house. Danny, get that pumpkin outside and I will clean the table." It is truly remarkable how quickly four people can make a house presentable! Soon everything looked great, with the exception of the dirty dishes in the sink. We had a kitchen-den combination; there was no alternative to the visitors passing the kitchen sink, which was now laden with dirty dishes.

I am grateful to report God still speaks today; He spoke in my mind, "Put the dirty dishes in the oven!" Why didn't I think of that? I rushed to the sink and shuffled the dishes to the oven. My house now looked like something out of *Better Homes and Gardens*. Soon the visitors came and were welcomed into a sparkling, clean house.

After talking a few minutes, it became evident these two women were special and I immediately liked them. Conversation was easy and my five-year-old daughter, Jenise, was impressed they lived on a farm. She was invited to go home with them and, of course, she was ready. As soon as the car door shut, Jenise fell against the passenger window and said, "WHEW!" Mrs. Gill asked, "Honey, what is wrong?" Jenise could not speak clearly and she tiredly replied, "Ever since you called, my mama make me wuk and wuk. Me and Jeff take the shoes and the coats and the newspapers and we throw them on Jeff's bed and shut the doe." Then she got a questioning look on her face and said, "BUT MAMA PUT THE DIRTY DISHES IN THE OVEN!" Immediately the sham of a clean house was exposed; my secret was out. In spite of my deception, Mrs. Gill and Sandra had a great sense of humor and became my adopted family during my time in Memphis.

Regardless of how clean my house looked, truth revealed the hidden things. As Christians, we often appear pious when our hearts are permeated with unforgiven sin. When God's holy light is allowed to shine in the deepest places of our heart, we see pockets of darkness. What does the truth of the Holy Spirit want to reveal about the hidden sins in your life? Are you willing to acknowledge these sins and clean out the recesses of your mind and heart?

- Is there anyone you have not forgiven?
- Do you envy another's possessions?
- Do you have a negative attitude?
- Are you easily discouraged?
- Do you tell "little white lies?"
- Do you gossip?
- Is your mind set on "the things of the earth?"
- Are you selfish with your money and time?
- Is there anyone you would like to see fail?
- Does a carnal nature plague you?
- Do you easily become angry?
- Are you ever harsh with people?
- Do you have a lack of concern for the lost?
- Are you spiritually cold?

Hidden sin prevents us from living in close communion with God and others; these sins have a way of coming to the surface at unforeseen times. It is imperative for Christians to reflect Jesus Christ if others are to be drawn to Him. Non-Christians need to witness disciples of Jesus whose lives are different from their own. We possess the Living Water but it can become tainted with sin and no longer desirable for the thirst of an unbeliever.

Archie King, a long-time pastor, tells a boyhood story of being hired to work on a farm. The days were long, hot and difficult. Several older workers passed a water jar, each taking a drink. However, by the time the jar reached Archie, the water was dirty and murky. He said, "I was hot and thirsty but I would rather have no water than bad water." Are we exhibiting "bad water" to our lost friends, family and co-workers due to the sin in our lives? The great news of the gospel is God's forgiveness; our hearts can be clean before Almighty God and His Spirit enables us to break the sin cycle of our humanity.

"If we walk in the light as He Himself is in the light, we have fellowship with one another, and the blood of Jesus His Son cleanses us from all sin." (I John 1:7)

Stepping into the Light

When darkness is overcome by God's light of forgiveness, our lives become a beacon of God's grace. His gift of forgiveness is complete and final; we must in turn forgive ourselves for the hurt we have caused others.

Are you tired of pious but ordinary living? Step into the light of His mercy and forgiveness!

The Holy Spirit dispels the darkness. God desires to use all events of our lives for His glory and He can bring good from any situation. He has given Christians a supernatural element that can enable us to rise above our circumstances. We must remember this present darkness is not permanent because God's word tells us, **"joy comes in the morning!"** If you have experienced a dark time in your life, seek God's guidance in turning darkness into light. Regardless of the reason for the pain, God responds with a promise.

"The Spirit also helps our weakness; for we do not know how to pray as we should, but the Spirit Himself intercedes for us with groanings too deep for words; and He who searches the hearts knows what the mind of the Spirit is, because He intercedes for the saints according to the will of God." (Romans 8:26-27)

Dave Dravecky was a major league baseball pitcher who in 1988, was at the top of his game. He realized his childhood dream of playing professional baseball and life was certainly going his way. However, at the peak of his career, cancer was discovered in his pitching arm, forcing the removal of half the deltoid muscle. After the surgery, Dave went through rehab and vowed to return to baseball. The next year, he defied the odds and came back to pitch again. People in the stands were cheering and I watched the game on television in sheer amazement. He won the game and I remember crying as players of both teams swarmed him.

The next game Dave Dravecky pitched was a complete reversal of the celebration. It has been said he threw the "pitch that could be heard round the world." Dave's arm split in two and we watched him writhing in pain on the pitcher's mound. The fans began sobbing and even the sportscasters became emotional. Again, I remember crying and wondering why God allowed this dedicated, Christian man to undergo such heartbreak. Eventually, Dave's arm, along with his shoulder blade and collarbone, had to be amputated. His dream of playing professional baseball was crushed, his health was diminished, and all seemed lost. He says, "Little did I know that the dream I had since I was a little boy was simply a platform for sharing hope and faith with suffering people around the world." He and his wife founded Dave Dravecky's Outreach of Hope, a nonprofit organization for cancer patients. He speaks often of the strength found in Christ and is evangelistic in his messages. He has reached far more people for the Lord in his sickness than he ever would have in health.

Dave has a great perspective on suffering, "In America, Christians pray for the burden of suffering to be lifted from their backs. In the rest of the world, Christians pray for stronger backs so they can bear their suffering. It's why we look away from the bag lady on the street and to the displays in the store windows. It is why we prefer going to the movies instead of to hospitals and nursing homes." Dave Dravecky learned to step out of the darkness and into the light of God's perfect plan because he chose to embrace suffering.

What about your life? Has it taken some turns that brought disappointment, pain and disillusionment? *You will learn through suffering what you can never learn through success.* C. S. Lewis said it well, "God whispers to us in our pleasures, speaks in our conscience, but shouts in our pain." Listen to God speaking and you will find yourself taking the next step on the lighted path.

The Holy Spirit Comforts. A great blessing for the suffering Christian is to know after the darkness comes light and after pain comes comfort. God allows His children to experience brokenness, not only due to sin, but also from sickness and other reversals of life. He uses these situations to bring us to a state of being humble, surrendered and dependant. Thankfully, in His grace, He does not leave us where we are; He comforts and revives us. *God does not want us to remain crushed and lowly; he wants us to become committed and loving.* During heartbreaking times, we can experience God's presence and comfort at a deep level. The choice is ours to receive comfort from the Great Comforter. We can choose to become bitter and defeated or we can choose inner healing, joy, and peace.

"But the Helper, the Holy Spirit, whom the Father will send in My name, He will teach you all things, and bring to your remembrance all that I said to you. Peace I leave with you; My peace I give to you; not as the world gives, do I give to you. Do not let not your heart be troubled, nor let it be fearful." (John 14:26-27)

Recently, while driving, I needed to change lanes and glanced at my rear-view mirrors to assess the traffic. I made a mental note of the message on the passenger side mirror, "Objects are closer than they appear." I changed lanes; taking into consideration the mirror gave a confusing and distorted picture of the traffic's location. As we travel through life's complexities, we must remember, "God is closer than He appears." The heartache we experience may be confusing and God seems far away at times. Our pain can push our faith to a frightening point.

- Is God aware of my situation?
- Does He care?
- What is going to happen?
- Will He help me?

The truth is, "GOD IS ALWAYS CLOSER THAN HE APPEARS." Despite our confusion, if we reach out and grasp His outstretched hand, we will find comfort, peace, and strength for our souls. God's comfort through the Holy Spirit brings light into the darkest of places; we find ourselves walking a guided path to wholeness.

The Holy Spirit makes me a comforter. God miraculously turns our troubles into opportunities for service in His kingdom. When we have experienced, survived and grown through wrenching emotional or physical pain, we are better equipped to give comfort to another suffering soul. Someone has said, "God does not comfort us to make us comfortable but to make us comforters."

"Blessed be the God and Father of our Lord Jesus Christ, the Father of mercies and God of all comfort, who comforts us in all our afflictions so that we may be able to comfort those who are in any affliction with the comfort with which we ourselves are comforted by God." (II Corinthians 1:3-4)

When God has comforted a Christian, she can then comfort others who **"are in any affliction."** It is not necessary to suffer in the same manner for us to be able to bring a word of encouragement, counsel, or comfort. God desires for our trials to develop tender hearts-hearts that yearn to become comforters.

A little girl came home from a neighbor's house where her best friend had died. "Why did you go there?" questioned her father. "To comfort her mother," said the child. What could you do to comfort her?" asked the father. The girl replied, "I climbed up in her lap and cried with her." Are you willing to have a burdened heart on behalf of another?

Although God can use anyone as a comforter, there is a special empathy between people who have experienced the same pain; support groups are a testimony to this fact. Be good stewards of your pain; allow God to guide your path to someone who needs the strength you have gained. Your comfort brings with it a unique blend of compassion, patience, and understanding.

Once during Queen Victoria's reign, she heard the wife of a common laborer had lost her baby. Having experienced the deep loss of a child herself, she felt moved to personally express her sympathy. She visited the woman one day and spent some time with her. After she left, the neighbors asked the woman what the Queen said. "Nothing," replied the grieving woman, "she simply put her hands on mine and we silently wept together."

Do not be concerned about the mechanics of comforting; God will teach you what to do. It is not difficult; most suffering people simply want someone who cares. *Often the best comfort is tears, not talk.* If you have experienced a specific painful situation, watch for God's guidance to be used in His service; be willing to cry and show compassion. As you help another see God's light in the darkness, your path toward victory becomes clearer also.

Filled to overflowing. Every Christian receives the Holy Spirit when they accept Jesus Christ as their Savior. *They possess the Holy Spirit but the Holy Spirit may not possess them.* D. L. Moody said, "I believe firmly that the moment our hearts are emptied of pride, selfishness, ambition and everything that is contrary to God's law, the Holy Spirit will fill every corner of our hearts. But if we are full of pride, conceit, ambition and the world, there is no room for the Spirit of God. We must be emptied before we can be filled."

Do you want to be filled with the Spirit to overflowing? There is a great difference in a glass being filled with water and one being filled to overflowing. The overflowing glass can no longer contain the water and other things are affected. The same is true of the Christian life; when we are filled with the Holy Spirit to overflowing, God affects other people. The Spirit is not contained in us but is shared with others.

Andrew Murray said, "May not a single moment of my life be spent outside the light, love, and joy of God's presence and not a moment without the entire surrender of my self as a vessel for Him to fill full of His Spirit and His love." Are you willing to entirely surrender yourself in order to be filled with the Holy Spirit? You can become a victorious vessel as God fills and uses you to share His love with lost and hurting people.

There is a guide who lives in the deserts of Arabia and he has never lost his way. He carries with him a homing pigeon with a fine cord attached to one of its legs. When in doubt as to which path to take, the guide throws the bird into the air. The pigeon quickly strains at the cord to fly in the direction of home and thus leads the guide accurately to his goal. Because of this unique practice he is known as "the dove man."

The Holy Spirit, often identified in scripture as a dove, is willing and able to guide us on the path that leads to a more abundant life; we become victorious vessels when we submit to His all-knowing directions. He is fully capable of leading us along life's way.

Walk a Godly Path

"You are the light of the world. A city set on a hill cannot be hidden, nor do men light a lamp and put it under the peck-measure, but on the lamp stand; and it gives light to all who are in the house. Let your light shine before men in such a way that they may see your good works and glorify your Father who is in heaven." (Matthew 5:14-16)

How can we be the light that guides others to the Father? Our lives must bear a close resemblance to Jesus Christ; the characteristics of His life should be exemplified in our lives. "**Christ in you, the hope of glory.**" **(Colossians 1:27b)** As Christians, we take the name of Jesus Christ and also the responsibility to live "Christ like."

As a teenager, my Dad consistently told me to behave in such a way I would bring no dishonor to the family name. How much more should we diligently strive to bring no dishonor to the heavenly family name? In fact, we should constantly work to bring honor to our Lord. Unfortunately, we often become complacent in our spiritual growth; we intend to be ready for the "big task" but until then, we plateau in our spiritual life. The Christian life is too important to be taken casually; lost and hurting people are waiting to see Christ in someone they know. Thomas Carlyle said, "Our business is not to see what lies dimly at a distance but to do what lies clearly at hand."

Several years ago, my family and I moved to Murfreesboro, Tennessee, and bought a house in the country. Eventually several houses were built around us and we learned to love our new neighbors. One house in particular sold numerous times until a family moved in and said they were staying for the long term. I remember inviting this family to my church two times and I never asked again. I did not want to push my "religion" on them and hinder our new relationship.

This family had a little boy named Kelly; he was nine-years old and cute as could be. He won my heart immediately and he knew it. Every time Kelly saw me in the backyard, he ran over and began talking. He liked to mow the lawn and his special love was fireworks. I watched Kelly grow up into a fine, young man; at nineteen-years old, he was handsome and had a winning personality. Kelly seemed to have life by the tail; playing sports, dating, and starting college.

One summer day, Kelly's father ran to my back door and yelled for help. He said, "Come quick, Bessie needs you." As he turned to run home, I asked, "What is wrong?" He said sobbing, "Kelly has killed himself." I could not believe my ears; I could not believe the little boy who loved to play, talk and shoot fireworks was gone.

I sat with Bessie, Kelly's mother, and tried to console her. Her mother's heart had been ripped apart and there was little I could do. We sat and cried together, wondering what could have made Kelly so desperate. I realized in ten years of talking to Kelly, I had never spoken to him about the Lord or how God gives strength when we need it. Although I attended church every time the doors were opened, I failed to minister to a hurting, young man at my own back door. Would it have made a difference in Kelly's life if I had talked with him about the strength God gives? I do not know, but I would have the assurance of having tried.

Kelly's memory is still fresh on my mind, even though it has been eight years since he left us. Mentally I still see him riding the lawn mower and flashing his brilliant smile. At the same time, his memory challenges me to be more aware of opportunities God gives me to encourage, minister and give a witness of God's love. I do not want another Kelly in my life, someone for whom I fail to minister. I do not want a Kelly in your life either. God has placed people in our realm of relationships that need to see Jesus through our words and actions. Living an extraordinary life, one filled with the characteristics of Christ, does not come easily. We will fail; we will have regrets; we must learn from our mistakes. Will we be found faithful? Will we consciously cultivate the actions and attitudes of Christ?

In recent years, a catch phrase in schools has been, "Character Counts." The character of Christians counts for eternity. Our actions may seem unimportant at the time but as a stone thrown into a pond causes ripples, so our lives affect others, either negatively or positively. The "ripples" are caused most often by small acts rather than the "big task" God may someday call us to accomplish. If we are to walk a Godly path, we need to evaluate where we are on our journey.

- Are you concerned about God using you daily in His Kingdom's work?
- Are others inspired by your life?
- Can anyone see a "family resemblance" of Christ in you?
- Do you have a major character flaw?
- Are you willing to be remade into the likeness of Christ?

Christ's Characteristics

Humility. Jesus was God incarnate, sinless and all knowing, yet He remained approachable to everyone. Although He had every right to exalt himself, He displayed humility in all instances. He was born in a smelly manger, worked as a lowly carpenter, was a homeless adult, died as a criminal and was buried in a borrowed grave.

"And being found in appearance as a man, He humbled Himself by becoming obedient to the point of death, even death on the cross." (Philippians 2:8)

As followers of Jesus Christ, arrogance and pride should have no part in our lives. We, of all people, know the depravity of our sin and the grace required from God to save us. As we reflect on God's grace, we should stand humbled before the Lord.

When Ann and I were in Iran, our guide was a dedicated Muslim and proficient in the English language. He had no problem translating between Farsi and English. However, at an impromptu worship service in a closed Christian church, Ann mentioned the word, "grace." Our guide stumbled and stuttered in the translation; finally, he obviously skipped the word. Afterward, we asked why he had difficulty in translating the word, "grace." He replied, "There is no such word in the Farsi language. A man works for what he gets from Allah. He earns it or he does not earn it; either way, it is what a man does that counts." Such a mind-set is filled with pride. However, Christians often exalt themselves through work, finances and accomplishments. We also use our families and religious activities as objects of pride. We begin to think we have earned our blessings from hard work and business acumen. God's word urges us to be humble before the Lord and in the presence of others. Only then can He use us to the fullest.

"Clothe yourselves with humility toward one another, for God is opposed to the proud but gives grace to the humble. Humble yourselves, therefore, under the mighty hand of God, that He may exalt you at the proper time." (I Peter 5:5b-6)

Generosity. Christ had very little but He shared what He had. Even though He could have turned stones into bread, He was content with the standard of living the Father chose for Him. He generously shared his time, friendship, and food. Americans have much to learn about contentment and generosity; few are content with their standard of living and although they give money to charities, it is small in comparison to what they spend on themselves. This seems to be the accepted rule.

A rare exception was a man named Dick Kleinau. He visited my Sunday school class the morning we began a new project of sending our church's used literature to Africa. Afterward, he asked if it would be acceptable for a visitor to donate some money for the expenses. I accepted his offer and he quietly wrote a check for $1,000. Dick was not an extremely wealthy man because, in his words, "God has given me the ability to make money in order for me to give it away." He was anonymous in his generosity and wanted no recognition.

One day Dick asked me to pray with him about a vision he had from the Lord. His daughter, who was a nurse, saw many families of children with special needs being turned away from outpatient facilities because they could not afford to pay the bills. Dick and his daughter envisioned a facility where medically fragile children and those with special needs would not be turned away. Instead they would be embraced with Christian love and healing arms, regardless of their family's financial situation.

Dick was consumed with God's vision and began taking necessary steps to see it become a reality. He and his wife, Angie, sold their boat, although it was a favorite place for family outings. From this sale and other funds, Dick sacrificially provided the financing that enabled a facility to be built debt free in 1998; it was named Special Kids and dedicated to the Lord.

Unfortunately, Dick never saw the fruit of his labor; he passed away a month before the opening of Special Kids. However, his vision and generosity lives on in the ministry to children with severe handicaps. Over 1,200 families have been served and the message of Jesus Christ is shared freely with the children and their extended families. Recently, a Special Kids facility was opened in China. Due to the unselfishness of one man, God is touching special children with His love. Because of Dick's obedience, others now have the opportunity to continue the ministry through giving and serving.

- Are you generous with your possessions?
- Would you sell something very important to you for the good of someone you do not know?
- Is God glorified through your finances?
- Are you generous with your time?

Flexibility. The gospels relate many situations where Jesus' plans were changed because of human need; his itinerary was open to interruptions. However, we find ourselves scheduling God out of our day. We are busy, distracted and unconcerned, but God has plans for His children to minister "as they go." Becoming more aware of His presence in our life, we learn to adjust our agenda to His will. God walks with us, tells us what to say and shows us the person for whom we are to minister. Following His direction, we find opportunities to share our faith and His love. The divine appointments may be quite unexpected but the Lord has a purpose in placing people, especially lost people, in our path. *We must allow sacred stops in our busy schedule.*

Ann and I attended an interdenominational women's prayer meeting at a local church and were on our way to lunch. We planned to have a leisurely meal before Ann attended a scheduled meeting. Traffic was heavy in the downtown area and although we had sufficient time to complete our plans, I was impatient. Coming to a four-way intersection, I stopped behind an older van. A man was driving but when it was his time to go, he did not move. This increased my level of impatience but I held my tongue since I had only minutes before left the prayer meeting. Three other cars crossed the intersection but the van remained still. I said aloud in an irritated tone, "WELL, GO ON!" (I do not know what I would have said if I had not attended the prayer meeting.) Staring at the man, I saw him move to the back of the van. I said to Ann, "Now if that is not just like a man; he has parked and is going to unload something. I can't believe he is blocking this entire intersection."

Suddenly the side of the van opened and the driver lowered himself onto the street in a wheelchair. He was a young paraplegic and guilt gripped my heart. He rolled the wheelchair to the back of the van and looked at it helplessly. Ann and I asked if there was anything we could do and he said he needed a tow truck. During the time I was making arrangements for the truck, a man approached the van. When I finished the call, Ann said, "Look at that guy, he must be a Pentecostal preacher." He was wearing a white shirt and had long, gray hair; he was talking with the young man, pointing to the sky and clapping his hands. Yes, he looked like a Pentecostal preacher all right. (We learned later he was a music minister at a nearby Baptist church.)

As we returned to the young man, the minister clapped his hands and said in a loud voice, "Son, if you die today, you are going to split hell wide open." The fellow in the wheelchair had a look on his face that said, "What in the world have I gotten into?" His eyes became bigger and bigger and he looked around for an escape. I whispered to the minister and asked the young man's name. "I don't know," was his reply. (Ann says you really need to know a person's name before you tell them they are going to split hell wide open!)

We learned his name was Bill; he was a twenty-three-year-old student at the local university. I asked, "Bill, are you a Christian?" He responded, "No, but I am not ready yet." This statement rejuvenated the minister and he said sternly, "This is a divine appointment, these ladies are Christians and we are NOT going to let you go until you accept Jesus Christ." Bill looked at us as helplessly as he had earlier looked at his broken-down van. Ann and I shared with Bill our testimony and explained how a person becomes a Christian. He thoughtfully said again, "I am just not ready yet." These words put new fire in the minister and he went on another rampage. Finally, Bill looked at us with a wide-eyed stare and asked, "When is that tow truck coming?"

As we left Bill, we gave him our card and told him we would be praying for him. Ann began to look in her purse as we drove away. I asked what she was doing and she replied, "I think we should pay Bill's tow charges." The same thought passed through my mind moments earlier so we knew this was the Spirit's prompting. Ann went to her meeting and I drove to the repair shop. After I paid the tow charge, the manager inquired, "When Bill asks who paid his bill, what do I say?" I reached for the invoice and wrote at the bottom, "Paid in full, as Jesus paid my sin debt and yours." Returning the invoice to the manager, I said, "He'll know."

I don't know if Bill ever accepted Christ as his Savior but Ann and I have prayed for him many times. I know God directed us to make a divine stop at the intersection to help a young man and tell him about the love of God. Unfortunately, I am certain we have missed other opportunities to minister because our schedule dictated our inaction. Will we listen to God's instruction and allow an interruption in our agenda? *When God speaks quietly, will we act quickly?*

Servant. Jesus was content to serve, even though He was the Master of all. He could have used his position for power and prestige but chose instead to promote others by serving them. He taught the disciples the importance of being a servant by washing their dirty feet, a job reserved for the lowest of slaves. It shocked the disciples when the Messiah completed this menial task but His message was clear.

"But Jesus called them to himself, and said, "You know that the rulers of the Gentiles lord it over them, and their great men exercise authority over them. It is not so among you, but whoever wishes to become great among you shall be your servant, and whoever wishes to be first among you shall be your slave." (Matthew 20:25-27)

Jesus left us an example by his actions; no task is beneath our dignity if God directs our participation. All of us would benefit from serving someone who can offer nothing in return. We never soar as high as when we serve the lowly and lonely.

Love, Compassion, Mercy, Gentleness. These characteristics of Christ should challenge our hearts to be more like our Lord. *Our depth of caring demonstrates our devotion and commitment to Christ.* If we have an intimate relationship with God, our heart will become more like His. Mercy and gentleness flow from a loving, compassionate heart. Christ rarely lost

His temper, He spoke harshly only to the self-righteous religious leaders and showed mercy and compassion to all. He looked beyond the problem to the person. Does your life touch people with love, compassion, mercy and gentleness?

My mother exemplifies these characteristics more clearly than any person I know. She is reserved in her personality but unrestrained in her actions as she demonstrates love with mercy and gentleness. She is ninety-two years old but if there were a death in the neighborhood today, she would be the first at the door to bring food and comfort. Her concern is shown through compassionate conduct.

During the Great Depression, my mother gave birth to her first child; a few days later, a neighbor also gave birth to her first child. As happens occasionally, the neighbor was unable to nurse her baby. There was no money to buy milk; the baby grew weak and lost weight. My mother walked across the field to visit the neighbor and the new baby girl. She saw a tiny baby who was crying of thirst and it broke my mother's heart. With the compassion of Christ, she offered to nurse this baby in order to keep her alive. Due to the fragile health of the baby, my mother made many trips across the field to give life-sustaining milk. The baby's health began to flourish and she survived because of the compassion and mercy of my mother. Today there is a seventy-year-old woman in Paris, Tennessee, who says she owes her life to my mother. As surely as the fragile baby needed physical nourishment years ago, there is someone around you whose life needs spiritual nourishment.

- Will you show the compassion and mercy of Christ to someone outside your family, even if it takes hours, weeks or years?
- Do you have a gentle spirit when dealing with others?
- Would you want God to give you mercy with the same measure you give mercy to others?

Prayerfulness. Jesus saw the need to spend quality time with His Father; it was a necessary part of his life. Crowds demanded his attention, the disciples wanted to hear him teach, and religious duties awaited; this did not prevent him from praying. Regardless of the busyness of the day, He found time to be alone with His Father.

"Immediately He made the disciples get into the boat and go ahead of Him to the other side, while He sent the crowds away. After He had sent the crowds away, He went up on the mountain by Himself to pray; and when it was evening, He was there alone." (Matthew 14:22-23)

170 Overcoming the Ordinary Life

"It was at this time that He went off to the mountain to pray, and He spent the whole night in prayer to God." (Luke 6:12)

It is foolish for us to think we can live the extraordinary life apart from a regular, in-depth prayer time. Someone has said, "If you are too busy to pray, you are too busy." Prayer should be as much a part of our life as breathing. Jesus talked with His Father until His last breath; may it be so with us.

Thankfulness. In good times and in difficult circumstances, gratitude and praise flowed from the heart and mouth of Jesus toward His Father. There is strength in a thankful spirit and gratitude changes our perspective during painful days. Dietrich Bonhoeffer said, "Gratitude changes the pangs of memory into a tranquil joy." Paul tells us, **"In everything give thanks; for this is God's will for you in Christ Jesus." (I Thessalonians 5:18)**

- Is your level of thankfulness dependant upon your blessings?
- Can you thank God for difficult times in your life or your children's lives?
- Do you thank God for everything?
- Do you give thanks spontaneously?

My grandson, Luke, was excited about Christmas; he was two years old and the holidays were a new experience. Luke has a definite taste for anything sweet, and Christmas brought an abundance of desserts and candy. He was also learning about the importance of Jesus coming into the world. To help him understand, his mom placed a small nativity scene in his bedroom; it became Luke's routine to kiss baby Jesus before and after bedtime. Nothing would deter him from this act of love.

Shortly before Christmas, Luke was in his bedroom with his mother as she folded clothes; suddenly he clasped his hands and began to pray. This was his first "real" prayer as he usually recited a child's prayer at bedtime and meals; this time it was spontaneous. He said, "OH-H-H LORD, thank you for baby Jesus and CAKE! Amen." Luke broke out in praise to God for what was important in his life. If our hearts were full of gratitude for the simple things, our perspective would be different and disappointments fewer.

On my first international mission trip, I realized how ungrateful I had been for God's blessings. Working in Venezuela, we were told never to drink the water or eat raw vegetables, and due to the lack of air conditioning, dress for the extremely hot weather. Because there was a water shortage, we were instructed to use only a small amount for our baths and never leave water running in the sink. I filled the bathtub with two inches of water and one inch was mud, slightly wet my toothbrush and turned the water off because of the shortage. I was extremely careful about what I ate and almost died from the heat. Returning home, I was grateful for clean water to drink, mud free baths, safe food to eat, and a climate controlled home. I do not let water run anymore while brushing my teeth, something I never thought about until that experience.

How long has it been since you thanked God for your car, clean water, healthy children, and food in your cabinets? There are a multitude of blessings for which we need to thank God. Would you take a few moments to spontaneously praise God for all His benefits to you?

Joy. Few have a mental picture of Jesus being joyful; he is usually portrayed as serious and even stern. People are rarely drawn to someone with this demeanor. However, Jesus consistently drew large crowds everywhere He went; children were comfortable in His presence. The reason? He was the essence of joy.

"These things I have spoken to you, that My joy may be in you and that your joy may be made full." (John 15:11)

Jesus instructed the disciples to be full of His joy. Can you honestly say you are full of joy? **"Do not be grieved, for the joy of the Lord is your strength." (Nehemiah 8:10c)** Christians can experience joy to the core of their being, even when life is at its worse. *Difficult circumstances should not lessen our joy; rather our joy should lighten our circumstances.* Jesus endured the cross **"for the joy set before him."** Life is much too precious to live in a somber and sad state.

Thomas Carlyle said, "Wondrous is the strength of cheerfulness and its power of endurance. The cheerful man will do more in the same time, will do it better, and will persevere in it longer, than the sad or sullen."

We know God has a reason for every event in life and His plans for us are good, therefore, we should display joy to the world. I am convinced the lack of joy in professing Christians is the greatest hindrance to nonbelievers coming to know the Lord. If we go about our daily duties with a joyful attitude, people would be drawn to the "Christ in us." It is time for us to allow the joy of the Lord to reign and demonstrate to the world we are living a victorious life!

Our influence is tremendous when we walk a Godly life, embodying the characteristics of Christ. Following Christ requires a commitment of everything we are, for every day we live; our walk is a process, one step at a time. We are guided by God and inspired by other dedicated, loyal Christians. Who influences you and whom are you influencing? Several years ago, I wrote the following as a tribute to those who have influenced my life.

Hands

My dad often talks about parental influence, including inherited traits; he is convinced children inherit the worst traits of their parents. My hands reveal this truth completely, short and wide like my dad's, wrinkled like my mother's. I look at my hands often and see theirs.

Mother's: Hands covered with sun spots from working in the garden and pulling grass from her flower beds, red and chapped from hanging the clothes to dry in freezing weather and rough from canning and freezing vegetables so her family could eat well in the winter. Hands that wiped away the tears of her three children, made the best biscuits anyone ever tasted, and rubbed our stomachs when we ate too many. These same hands took in a malnourished baby and saved its life, prepared food for every neighbor who had a death or sickness in the family, and bathed and soothed the running sores of a lonely woman. Hands that guided me to a deeper knowledge of Jesus by watching her life of love and commitment; these were gentle hands, more gentle than any I have ever known.

Daddy's: Strong hands that seventy years ago cut trees, sawed planks and personally built the home where he and my mother still live. Nails split and bleeding from cutting holes in the ice on the pond so the cattle could drink, skin dark in the summer from plowing in the fields from morning to night, hands calloused and dirty from hard work. These same hands worked long into the night harvesting the crops for a sick man in the community, hands quick to reach into his wallet and share what little he had with someone who had less. These were the hands I remember most; strong hands clasped in prayer before meals, praying for missionaries far from the doors of our country home. These hands in prayer taught me about the mission-heart of Jesus and His burden for the lost.

As I recall their hands, they somehow resemble other hands, dry from extreme heat, calloused from hard work, dirty from lack of water. These hands touched a leper, held a child and wiped tears at the death of His friend. These hands have nail prints, nail prints in sacrifice for my salvation.

Yes, my hands are too short, too wide and wrinkled. But I pray my hands will exhibit the gentle, sacrificial and praying of the hands of my mother, daddy and Jesus.

Conclusion

In recent days our nation has experienced the loss of former President Gerald R. Ford. His presidency was unusual because he is the only U.S. President who was not elected. He was actually appointed to the vice presidency by Richard Nixon before he ultimately assumed the presidency at Nixon's resignation. Betty Ford said of their life, "We are ordinary people who found ourselves in extraordinary circumstances."

So it is with the Christian life. God has chosen to populate His Kingdom with a host of ordinary people whom He intends to use in extraordinary ways. He orchestrates adventures of ministry, service, and love for us, His children, which exceed anything the world has to offer. The world system erects barriers to our faith walk – barriers of conformity, fear, greed, and religious retreat. Are you tired of ordinary living, being average, having low expectations and mediocre accomplishments? God will grant the victory if we will simply obey His commands, listen to His voice, and radically follow the example Jesus set before us during His life on earth. There are great blessings beyond the barriers of ordinary living!

"The thief comes only to steal and kill and destroy; I came that they may have life, and have it abundantly." (John 10:10)

Study Questions

Chapter 1: CONFORMITY'S CURSE

1. Why do you think God used the illustration of a potter to explain His dealings with His people? (Jeremiah 18:1-6)
2. What is the difference between conformity and transformation? (Romans 12:2)
3. Does conformity to society's value system prevent spiritual renewal? How?
4. What does it mean to become a new creature in Christ? (II Corinthians 5:17)
5. Do you believe God can remold your life and change the outcome?
6. Is it necessary for God to bring crushing circumstances to change a life?
7. How does compliance to God's purposes affect the length of the molding process of the Potter?
8. What steps can you take to deepen the level of your commitment to God's purposes? What are some of God's methods for increasing a believer's desire for His will?

Chapter 2: FEAR FACTOR

1. Why is fear a recurring problem in the lives of many people today?
2. Do you agree with the statement, "Situational fear is a trust issue?" Why or why not?
3. Does seeking God's perspective on circumstances help an individual deal with fear? How?
4. How does faith in God's promises destroy anxiety and fear?
5. List several of God's promises especially meaningful in your spiritual pilgrimage. How can belief in God's promises provide security for daily living?

6. List the five steps in Section 2 that guide a believer out of the pit of worry. Give a brief explanation of each step and how it applies to a current source of worry in your life.
7. What is involved in surrendering your problems into God's hands?
8. Describe a time when the peace of God flooded your mind during a difficult time.

Chapter 3: GREED'S GRASP

1. What is the difference between spiritual abundance and simple affluence? Can both be experienced simultaneously? Which do you prefer?
2. What factors in society predispose Christians to the temptation of greed? List other areas of greed in addition to money.
3. List some of the common objections to ministry. Discuss ways to overcome each objection.
4. What are three outcomes from ministry the writer discusses? Can you think of other possible outcomes?
5. Do you agree with the statement, "We want out lives touched but our lifestyles left unchanged?" Why or why not?
6. What should be our reaction when faced with overwhelming hurts and needs?
7. Explain the difference between passive service and passionate sharing.
8. What needy situation has God brought to your attention during this study? How will you react?

Chapter 4: RELIGIOUS RETREAT

1. How should Christians react to our increasingly secular society? Is attendance at your church growing or declining? Why?
2. What are the characteristics of hyper-religious people?
3. There are four characters in *The Good Samaritan* Story. With which character do you identify? Explain.
4. What is a working definition of the word *compassion*? Why does real compassion result in ministry?
5. What are Jesus' two primary directives to people? Share a scripture for each.
6. What three places do the scriptures command us to dare to go? Is there someone God placed upon your heart as you studied this chapter? Will you go?
7. On pages 127-129, what three attributes are outlined to escape religious retreat and walk in divine adventure?
8. Most Christians have difficulty sharing their faith. Why?

Chapter 5: VICTORIOUS VESSELS

1. How do you define prayer? What does the word *relationship* have to do with prayer?
2. On pages 139-143, the writer outlines three requests on the inward journey of prayer. List them and explain what each means to you personally.
3. Do you believe intercessory prayer can affect an unbeliever? What are three prayer requests listed for unbelievers? Can you think of others?
4. Witnessing is talking about God. What are two suggestions the writer offers to naturally share Christ?
5. Describe a time when God seemed far away. Describe a time when He seemed very near. What factors determined your perception of God during these times? How can both experiences be a part of your Christian testimony?
6. List the characteristics of Christ found on pages 164-171. Does your life exemplify these characteristics? On each of these, rate yourself on a scale of 1-10.
7. Who has been your greatest spiritual influence? Who is in your sphere of influence? What changes do you need to make in order for your life to be a positive influence on those around you?
8. Are you willing to allow God to take total control of your life? Are you ready for a spiritual adventure with the Lord? Pray that God will make you a victorious vessel that receives His blessings and pours them out on others.